Verse
by
Verse

A Devotional Commentary

through

James and Jude

(The half-brothers of our Lord)

Verse by Verse

A Devotional Commentary
through
James and Jude
(The half-brothers of our Lord)

by Dr. Ricky Gravley Jr.

Word of His Mouth Publishers
Mooresboro, NC

All Scripture quotations are taken from the **King James Version** of the Bible.

ISBN: 978-1-941039-65-6
Printed in the United States of America
© 2025 by Dr. Ricky Gravley

Word of His Mouth Publishers
Mooresboro, NC
www.wordofhismouth.com

Introduction

The devotionals in this book are a compilation of emails sent out every Monday morning on our church website. I entitled the book "Verse by Verse" because I would take one verse and write a short devotional from that verse every week. I did not write it in commentary form, but I would take a thought or phrase from the text and build upon it. I trust and pray that you will read something from each devotional that will help strengthen your Christian walk.

Devotional books have always inspired me to meditate more on His Word, and they have challenged me to examine the text more closely to find the little hidden gems within each verse. I hope this edition of Verse by Verse will benefit you as you read through the books of James and Jude.

Dedication

I dedicate this book to my youngest daughter, Celestial Hardeman, who has always been a great blessing to me. I am very thankful for her love for Christ and her dedication as she follows her husband and seeks God's will for her life. I have observed her as a faithful wife to her husband and a loving mother to her children. She has brought great joy and laughter to our lives as her parents.

Celest, I love you dearly, and I am thankful that the Lord has blessed you and your family.

Table of Contents

James 1 15

    Who Am I 17

    Joy for the Journey 18

    Knowing Patience 19

    God's Goal for Your Life 20

    The Perfect Prayer 21

    Going Against the Tide 22

    Don't Leave Empty Handed 24

    Make Up Your Mind 26

    Treasures Unseen 27

    How the Rich Become Poor 29

    Where Are They Now 30

    A Beatitude for the Right Attitude 32

    Don't Blame God 34

    Defining the Moment 36

    The Deadly Triangle of Sin 37

    Do Not Go Astray 39

    The Gifts of God 40

    The New Birth 41

    The Mature Saints 42

    It Doesn't Work 43

    The Soil of the Soul 45

    A Doer or a Deceiver? 46

    God's Looking Glass 47

    He Has No Idea 49

    How to be Blessed 51

    Vain Religion 52

    Pure Religion 54

James 2 56

    Pyramid Climbers 58

    The Two Visitors 59

The Snooty Usher 61
What Right Do We Have? 62
A Tremendous Truth 63
The Church Bully 65
It Still Happens Today 66
The Royal Law 67
Discrimination Biblically Defined 68
Lawbreakers 69
Good Deeds Will Not Do 70
How Did You Use Your Liberty Today? 71
A Fair Trial or Free Pardon? 72
Balancing the Scale 73
The Poor and Needy 75
A Worthless Prayer 76
Dead Faith 78
What Good is Dead Faith? 79
A Demonic Faith 81
The Empty Man 82
Is Your Isaac on the Altar? 84
Partners Together 85
The Friend of God 86
A Faith that Works 88
She God Saved 89
Dead Clay 90

James 3 91
The Sunday School Teacher, Pt 1 93
The Sunday School Teacher, Pt 2 94
The Bridle 95
The Bit 96
The Boat 98
The Boaster 99
The Fiery Tongue 100
A Wild Tongue 102
An Evil Tongue 103

A Double Tongue 104

A Hypocritical Tongue 105

The Spring of the Soul 106

A Simple Fact 107

Knowledge vs Wisdom 109

Self-Promotion Pt 1 110

Self-Promotion Pt 2 111

Confusion Baptist Church 112

Heavenly Wisdom 114

The Peacemaker 115

James 4 116

Believer vs Believer 118

The Battle Royal 120

Unanswered Prayers 122

Spiritual Adultery 123

The Flesh 124

More Grace 125

Satan on the Run 126

Draw Me Nearer 127

Real Repentance 128

The Way Up Is Down 129

Evil Speaking 131

Do You Know the Judge? 133

The Perfect Plan 134

What Is Your Life? 135

Acknowledging the Almighty 137

The Wrong Kind of Rejoicing 138

The Definition of Sin 139

James 5 140

The Tears of Rich Men 142

Rusty Gold and Tattered Garments 143

The Witness of Wealth 144

The lord of Sabaoth 145

The Price of Pleasure...146
The Death of the Righteous.......................................147
Wait for the Rain 149
We Are Getting Closer 150
The Judge Standeth at the Door..................................151
Prophet or Puppet 153
The Patience of Job 155
The Poer of Yes and No 157
Suffering and Song...158
The Elders of the Church...159
The Prayer of Faith...160
The Man of Prayer..161
The Earnest Prayer 162
The Second Prayer..164
A Backslidden Brother 165
A Heart for the Wayward 166

Jude 168
Jude, the Brother of James..171
God's Multiplication 172
Earnestly Contend for the Faith.................................173
The Creepy Old Men of Apostasy..............................174
You Already Know This 176
The Imprisonment of Angels.....................................177
Strange Flesh 179
Filthy Dreamers 180
Facing the Devil 181
Brute Beasts..182
Mark These Men..184
Some People Have No Shame.....................................186
The Great Tsunami 187
A Bright Word in a Dark Hour...................................189
Judgment Day!...191
The Profile of an Apostate...193
Words to Remember..195

God's Men Told Us Right 197
Having Not the Spirit.. 199
Praying in the Hoy Ghost 201
An Absolute Must... 203
You Can Make a Difference................................... 205
Be Careful in the Rescue 207
How to Keep From Falling..................................... 209
Our Wise God... 211
Notes 213

James 1

1 James, a servant of God and of the Lord Jesus Christ, to the twelve tribes which are scattered abroad, greeting.

2 My brethren, count it all joy when ye fall into divers temptations;

3 Knowing this, that the trying of your faith worketh patience.

4 But let patience have her perfect work, that ye may be perfect and entire, wanting nothing.

5 If any of you lack wisdom, let him ask of God, that giveth to all men liberally, and upbraideth not; and it shall be given him.

6 But let him ask in faith, nothing wavering. For he that wavereth is like a wave of the sea driven with the wind and tossed.

7 For let not that man think that he shall receive any thing of the Lord.

8 A double minded man is unstable in all his ways.

9 Let the brother of low degree rejoice in that he is exalted:

10 But the rich, in that he is made low: because as the flower of the grass he shall pass away.

11 For the sun is no sooner risen with a burning heat, but it withereth the grass, and the flower thereof falleth, and the grace of the fashion of it perisheth: so also shall the rich man fade away in his ways.

12 Blessed is the man that endureth temptation: for when he is tried, he shall receive the crown of life, which the Lord hath promised to them that love him.

13 Let no man say when he is tempted, I am tempted of God: for God cannot be tempted with evil, neither tempteth he any man:

14 But every man is tempted, when he is drawn away of his own lust, and enticed.

15 Then when lust hath conceived, it bringeth forth sin: and sin, when it is finished, bringeth forth death.

16 Do not err, my beloved brethren.

17 Every good gift and every perfect gift is from above, and cometh down from the Father of lights, with whom is no variableness, neither shadow of turning.

18 Of his own will begat he us with the word of truth, that we should be a kind of firstfruits of his creatures.

19 Wherefore, my beloved brethren, let every man be swift to hear, slow to speak, slow to wrath:

20 For the wrath of man worketh not the righteousness of God.

21 Wherefore lay apart all filthiness and superfluity of naughtiness, and receive with meekness the engrafted word, which is able to save your souls.

22 But be ye doers of the word, and not hearers only, deceiving your own selves.

23 For if any be a hearer of the word, and not a doer, he is like unto a man beholding his natural face in a glass:

24 For he beholdeth himself, and goeth his way, and straightway forgetteth what manner of man he was.

25 But whoso looketh into the perfect law of liberty, and continueth therein, he being not a forgetful hearer, but a doer of the work, this man shall be blessed in his deed.

26 If any man among you seem to be religious, and bridleth not his tongue, but deceiveth his own heart, this man's religion is vain.

27 Pure religion and undefiled before God and the Father is this, To visit the fatherless and widows in their affliction, and to keep himself unspotted from the world.

"Who Am I?"

James 1:1 - *"James, a servant of God and of the Lord Jesus Christ, to the twelve tribes which are scattered abroad, greeting."*

The first word of this Epistle gives us the identity of the author; his name is James. He was the son of Mary, the brother of the Lord Jesus, and the head of the Church in Jerusalem. These are important positions, but James does not mention any of them. He chooses the title, James, a servant.

The word "servant" is the Greek word "doulos," which is a bondservant. It means he was born a slave and has no personal freedom. A bondservant is obedient and devoted to his master. He depends upon him for daily provisions such as food, clothing, and shelter. James understands his role as a servant of God and the Lord Jesus Christ.

He also understands his responsibility. He is a servant to his master's people. In our verse, this refers to the twelve tribes of Israel. These are Jews living outside of Palestine. His was called to minister to the saints who were scattered abroad. He has a message of encouragement to help them in troublesome times. The word "greeting" means to rejoice or be glad.

We must take the time to remember our role and responsibility as Christians. We are servants of the Lord; called upon to reach the world with the Gospel, and minister to our fellow brethren. We are to give them a word of greeting and help them through the troublesome times of life. We are to be obedient and devoted servants who depend upon our Master for our daily provisions.

"Joy for the Journey"

James 1:2 - *"My brethren, count it all joy when ye fall into divers temptations;"*

Life does not always go our way. There are mountain tops to enjoy, and valleys to walk through, as we journey along. James understands that his brethren are not only scattered throughout the region, but that they are facing difficult times. They are going through times of testing.

In our verse, he uses the phrase, divers temptations. The word "divers" means various, and the word "temptations" refers to trials, or testings. We know that trials come in various forms and fashions. Each trial is unique within itself. James wants to encourage them that life for a Christian is not falling apart, but rather falling into place. Our responsibility is not to try to control the circumstances, but to control our spirit in the midst of trying circumstances. We must remain joyful, even when things do not turn out the way we plan.

James uses the word "count" in this verse. It is a financial term meaning "to evaluate." When trying times come to our doorstep, we must be determined to find the joy that is within us. There is a difference between joy and happiness. It is a fact that happiness comes from happenings, but joy comes from knowing Jesus. This is how a child of God can still have joy as he journeys along. He is not looking around at life, but he is looking at life from within.

God uses testing in life to mold us, make us, and mature us as we go along. Do not allow the things that you face to rob you of the joy that is within you. Do not allow the trials of life to pull you away from your relationship with Christ. You need Him more in the difficult times than ever before. Remember, if you will seek Him and trust Him, He will be with you and give you a song in the night. He will give you joy for the journey!

"Knowing Patience"

James 1:3 - *"Knowing this, that the trying of your faith worketh patience."*

If we are honest, there are some things we would rather not know about in life. There are even some people we would rather not have known in life. We cannot help but feel that life would be easier, less complicated, or less stressful if we could avoid certain issues, or certain people all together. Our flesh says that sometimes ignorance really is bliss.

If patience were a person, I think I would avoid her altogether. She would slow me down in my daily schedule. She would stress me out when I'm trying to finish a project or a goal that I have set. Patience would hinder me when my wants and desires are saying to me, "Buy this now, or go here today." She is always operating at a different pace, and the words "hurry" or "deadline" mean absolutely nothing to her.

The Bible says we need to know patience. The way we get to know patience is through the trials we face. Trials can slow us down and hinder our plans at times. They can even burden and break us to the point that we feel like we can't go on. God is using the pressure of the trial to strengthen our faith and bring patience to us. We learn to trust God more because patience is present. We may have tried to avoid her, and even ignored her at times, but she will not leave us. God knows how much we need her.

We do not appreciate her in everyday life, but when we are burdened down, or going through a trial, patience gives us hope. Patience tells us that God's promises will come to pass. Patience helps us to lean on the Lord when we cannot see what He is doing in our lives. Patience keeps us from giving up and helps us to go on. Patience becomes a good companion in the hard times of life. The more we know about patience, the more we know about God.

"God's Goal for Your Life"

James 1:4 - *"But let patience have her perfect work, that ye may be perfect and entire, wanting nothing."*

God's goal for our life is simple. He wants to make us complete in Him. He accomplishes this goal through His son, Jesus Christ. Christ works for us in Salvation. He then works in us by sanctification. Finally, He works through us in service. This is a process for the believer, a process that takes both time and patience.

Our verse teaches us to let patience have her perfect work. The word "perfect" indicates that the work has reached its end. It means it has been fully developed. I'm so thankful that the Lord doesn't leave us where He found us. He saves us, keeps us, and wants to develop us.

We have to be careful that we do not hinder the Lord's working in our life. God will not perform His work without our cooperation. We must yield our lives to Him. Daily and total surrender is the key to becoming a mature Christian lacking nothing.

In the end, this pleases both God and the believer. Like any good father, He knows what we need and what will make us happy. Think about your earthly father and how he was used to help mold you, and help make you into the person you are today. He had a goal for your life, and because of your obedience to him you are a better person today. When you failed to listen to his instructions, it only brought you hardship.

The same is true with our Heavenly Father. A patient child who is yielded to his Father will grow in maturity. He will not lack, because his Heavenly Father knows best. Surrender your life to God today, and allow him to accomplish His goal for your life.

"The Perfect Prayer"

James 1:5 - *"If any of you lack wisdom, let him ask of God, that giveth to all men liberally, and upbraideth not; and it shall be given him."*

Just because we develop into a more mature Christian, does not mean that we have all the answers. A mature Christian is not marked by how much they speak, but by how much they are able to control their speech. A child may say anything, at any time, to anyone. So it is with less mature saints. The more we learn, the more we realize how little we know.

James tells us that this is a problem for every believer. We face things in life every day that are beyond our wisdom and ability. We simply do not have the answers. We lack the wisdom that is needed for the circumstance.

James not only highlights the problem in this verse, but he also highlights the prayer. If you lack wisdom, then ask God for it. Do not try to figure it out yourself. Do not try to reason it over and over in your mind. You will go crazy if you do. If you try to discuss the problem over and over with someone else, then you will drive them crazy. What you need to do is pray for God to give you wisdom. After you have prayed, then wait for the answer.

Finally, James tells us about the promise. We are told in this verse that God will give you the answer. He will not keep it from you. The answer will be there when you need it. Do not fret today because you don't have the answers for tomorrow. The perfect prayer is, "Lord, I don't know what to do, and I need wisdom." Take your problem and turn it into a prayer, and then claim the promise in this verse. Hold to this promise, "and it shall be given you." God will not fail to give you the answer. He never has, and He never will. Trust Him for the wisdom that you need today.

"Going Against the Tide"

James 1:6 - "But let him ask in faith, nothing wavering. For he that wavereth is like a wave of the sea driven with the wind and tossed."

It can be so easy to develop the mindset, "just go with the flow." This seems to describe the world we are living in today. People are driven and tossed like a wave of the sea. They easily waver when it comes to culture, convictions and even Christianity. As the old saying goes, "they do not want to rock the boat." Why is it like this today? What is the underlying problem with society? Why have we traded patriots for pacifists? Why have we traded conviction for compromise?

Our verse tells us, that it goes back to the key elements of Christianity. It has everything to do with faith and prayer. Notice, the first phrase of our verse tells us to ask the Lord in faith, with nothing wavering. Whenever we seek the Lord in prayer, we should exercise complete trust in His Word. It is the prayer of faith that moves the hand of God. We cannot afford to waver in prayer. We cannot give doubt a moment's thought when laying our petition before Him.

We must go against the tide of doubt, and be firm in our faith. Faith builds character and conviction. Faith builds strength and confidence. It gives stability when things around us are being driven and tossed. Too many so called "Christians" today are like a wave on the sea. They allow anything to move them from where they stand, and what they believe. They are afraid to go against the tide, for fear of what others might say, or do.

My friend, if we are going to see our prayers answered, and find God's wisdom and direction in prayer, it is going to take faith that does not waver when the winds of this world blow against us. If we will stand firm on our knees in prayer, we can stand firm in a world that is vastly sinking.

"Don't Leave Empty Handed"

James 1:7 - *"For let not that man think that he shall receive any thing of the Lord."*

I have often said, "The Lord does not answer prayer based on merit, but on mercy." God is a merciful Father who loves us and invites us into His presence. He desires to fellowship with us, and hear what is on our hearts.

He knows our weakness and our frame. He knows we are the dust of this earth. He knows that we need a daily cleansing by His Word. He knows that we will stumble along the way, and that we need His forgiveness. He knows that no matter how hard we strive, we are going to come up short.

Now, just because the Lord understands who we are, does not mean He gives us a license to sin. Sin will hinder our prayer life. He will deal with our disobedience. However, God knows that our prayers are not based on our goodness, but on His goodness. He is good to answer us, but He wants one thing from us, above all else, that we exercise faith!

God wants us to fully trust Him when we speak to Him in prayer. Don't misunderstand what I'm saying when I make this statement. The Lord is willing to work with a lot of imperfections in our lives when He sees faith in our hearts. How many times has He answered a prayer for you when you knew you didn't deserve it? You are probably thinking every time. That's because He is merciful, and He saw faith in your life. He knew that you trusted Him in spite of yourself.

The individual who prays in doubt will walk away empty-handed every time. Jesus taught us to have faith in God. We are not to have faith in ourselves or in our prayers. We are to place our faith in Him when we pray. You don't have to walk away empty-handed in your prayer life. Have faith in the merciful hand of God, knowing that He will answer your prayer, not because you are good but because He is good!

"Make Up Your Mind"

James 1:8 - *"A double minded man is unstable in all his ways."*

The word for "double-minded" literally means "doubled soul." It describes a man who is divided in his loyalty. In fact, the Hebrew idiom is literally, "a heart and a heart." This is an individual who cannot make up his mind about where he stands, or what he believes. He struggles in his prayer life, therefore he has issues in every other aspect of life. He is a man who is unstable in all of his ways.

The word "unstable" means "to be restless." If an individual cannot be settled in prayer, then he will struggle in all other areas of life. Someone once said that "all failures are prayer failures." It is important that we seek wisdom from God daily. We must live in God's Word, and seek his will, in order to have a single mind.

So many people today are up and down. Society wants us to be open-minded. They want us to accept all people for who they are, and what they stand for. The Bible says the opposite. Friend, you must make up your mind which side of the aisle you are going to be on. Do not compromise or give in to this ever-changing world.

Think about a man standing in an airport who is double minded about whether or not he wants to get on the plane. He has purchased his ticket, and has made it through security. His flight has been called, and folks are boarding. If he stands there long enough, and does nothing, guess what happens? The gate will close, and the plane will push off from the terminal. He will have missed his flight. Even though he could not decide, the decision was made for him. If we do not seek God's counsel, we will not be ready when it comes time to make decisions in life. Friend, if you are not ready, then life will make those decisions for you. We must make up our minds. How? By daily asking God for wisdom.

"Treasures Unseen"

James 1:9 - *"Let the brother of low degree rejoice in that he is exalted:"*

James is encouraging these Jewish believers to look beyond their earthly standing and focus on their eternal standing. Persecution had driven many of them from their wealth and security. They had lost their jobs, their possessions, and their homes. They had become "brothers of low degree." They were people of humble circumstances. The word "low" means "low estate." Poverty was the common denominator among most of them, but they had riches that money could not buy. They had treasures unseen!

Though their earthly treasures were diminished, God had blessed them with eternal wealth. They were sons of God, joint heirs with the Lord Jesus! They were given the promise of heaven and sealed with the Holy Spirit! The Lord had exalted them, and had given them riches far above what this world could ever offer. James reminds them to rejoice!

This verse reminds me of an old song entitled, "I Found a Treasure When I Found Jesus." The riches of this world are like trash heaps when compared to the riches of eternity. Though the world cannot see it, and we cannot fully explain it, we rejoice in our position and glory in the promises of God! I'll gladly be called a brother of low degree in this world, to enjoy the splendor of the next world.

Child of God, do not concern yourself with riches or titles down here. They will mean nothing in eternity. You may not have great wealth, but if you know you are saved, then you have treasures unseen. You may not wear a fancy title or have a great position down here, but you are a child of the King for all eternity. When we take the focus off of where we stand here and place it on where we stand in Christ, then it will cause each of us to rejoice. He has lifted us up

27

out of the dung hills of this world and exalted us to the glories of Heaven. We are blessed with treasures unseen!

"How the Rich Become Poor"

James 1:10 - *"But the rich, in that he is made low: because as the flower of the grass he shall pass away."*

Poverty is not a sign of spirituality, any more than riches are a sign of sinfulness. This is not how the Lord measures men, and we should not either. Evil men are going to practice their evil ways regardless of whether they are rich or poor. A child of God that is right with his Heavenly Father will serve him, whether he is rich or poor.

However, we must not be fooled by riches. The only real security they can bring someone is a false security. Riches can be here today and gone tomorrow. This is also true about those who possess them. The question on my mind is, how do rich people become poor?

Some rich people become poor because they waste it. They have no discipline or common sense when it comes to spending. They may be rich, but they are poor stewards of what God has given them. Others lose their riches to tragedy, or things beyond their control. Circumstances can rob them of their wealth.

There are those that forsake their riches. They walk away from them to live a life of poverty, for a greater cause. We have all read of great missionaries who left family wealth, and forsook lucrative careers, to do the will of God. Then there are those who disobeyed the will of God. They chose a different path, and God chastised them with the loss of riches.

Finally, think of those who obtained wealth all of their life. They never knew poverty or hardship. They enjoyed a life of plenty, but one day death came calling, and they left it all behind. The truth of our text is that the rich die like the poor, and their riches are left behind. We are passing through this life and our soul, and the souls we lead to Jesus, is all we can take with us.

"Where Are They Now?"

James 1:11 - *"For the sun is no sooner risen with a burning heat, but it withereth the grass, and the flower thereof falleth, and the grace of the fashion of it perisheth: so also shall the rich man fade away in his ways."*

I recently read an article about the top 20 richest men who died in 2020. Among them were names such as: Joseph Safra (Brazilian citizen), who died in December at the age of 82, with a net worth of $23.2 billion; Whitney MacMillan (U.S. citizen), who died in March at the age of 90, with a net worth of $5.1 billion; and Randall Rollins (U.S. Citizen), who died in August at the age of 88, with a net worth of $4.7 billion.

The one who caught my attention the most, was Sumner Redstone. He also died in August of last year, at the age of 92. Redstone's net worth at death was $2.6 billion. He felt so empowered by his success, that in 2007 he told students at Boston University, "I'm in control now, and I'll be in control after I die." What a foolish statement!

Our verse talks about how the rich men of this world fade away. Where are they now? The rich man in Luke 16 is in Hell. The rich young ruler in Luke 18 is in Hell with him. In Luke 19, Zacchaeus was a rich man who got saved and is now in Heaven. One thing is for sure, riches do not last! They do not buy you one second longer on this earth when it comes time to die.

You see, every man's heart beats one beat at a time. The gain of worldly treasures cannot make it beat one second longer than God allows it. As the grass in the summer and the flower in the spring, we are here today, and gone tomorrow. Do not live for the riches of this life, live for the rewards of eternal life. Lay up treasures in Heaven, my friend. Focus on eternity, so that when it comes your time to die, not one family member, or friend, will ask the question, "Where are they now?"

"A Beatitude for the Right Attitude"

James 1:12 - *"Blessed is the man that endureth temptation: for when he is tried, he shall receive the crown of life, which the Lord hath promised to them that love him."*

The word "blessed" in our verse is the same word used in Matthew five. This word can mean "to make large" or "to be happy." However, it also carries a deeper meaning. It is used to describe an inner joy and satisfaction. The word "endure" carries the idea of waiting or exercising great patience. It means, "to bear up courageously."

Here we see a beatitude for the child of God that keeps the right attitude. Whenever we face the trials of life, it is our attitude that will determine whether or not we will make it through. The Lord promises inner joy and satisfaction to those who are willing to bear the trials of life courageously.

Think about this truth for a moment. There are those who have really never faced trials in life. Let's face it, they have had a pretty easy life. They have felt very little heartache and discomfort in life, yet they struggle to keep a right attitude. They constantly complain and grumble when things don't go the way they want them to. They constantly live a defeated life.

Then, there are others who have faced great trials and adversities in life. Through it all they seem to have constant joy. They very seldom, if ever, complain. These suffering saints speak of life with great joy and contentment. They faced the trial, passed the test, and live with the blessedness of God upon their life. All because they were willing to endure!

The Lord gives a blessing to help us in our test and a crown after we have passed our test! These are both coupled with a promise to those of us who love Him! We can choose to be blessed by God every day if we determine to take courage and bear the tests that we face with the right attitude.

"Don't Blame God"

James 1:13 - *"Let no man say when he is tempted, I am tempted of God: for God cannot be tempted with evil, neither tempteth he any man:"*

James goes from dealing with trials to dealing with temptations. The reason is because often times when trials come into our lives, the Devil sees that as an opportunity to tempt us. The Lord sends trials into our lives to bring the best out of us. Satan brings temptations into our lives to bring the worst out in us. The Lord's goal is to use trials to help us spiritually, while Satan's goal is to use temptation to help us to sin.

The best example of this would be the life of Job. The Lord was testing Job, but Satan was trying to tempt Job. God had a plan in the midst of Job's suffering, and so did Satan. Job had to make the choice as to how he was going to view his adversity. He could focus on the Lord, knowing that God would help him, or he could yield to Satan, and look for a way out by blaming God.

This was what Adam attempted that day in the garden, when he brought up the fact that the woman was given to him by God. While this was true, God was not to blame for Adam's sinful choice. God did not give Eve to Adam to tempt him to sin. What we say when we sin determines whether or not we find forgiveness for it. We must own our sin and be honest about it. We must be honest with ourselves, and before God.

There are also two great assurances in this verse. The first, is that we serve a God that can never be tempted to sin. He will never fall prey to the Devil! He is holy and cannot sin. The second, is that He would never tempt a man to commit sin. God is not interested in putting us in situations that will cause us to do wrong. He wants to make us stronger, so we can withstand the tempter. He always has

34

our best interest at heart. Rest today in knowing that our God will give us victory over sin and Satan.

"Defining the Moment"

James 1:14 - *"But every man is tempted, when he is drawn away of his own lust, and enticed."*

Our verse begins by telling us that every man is tempted. This is a fact that we all know and have experienced. No matter who you are or how long you have been serving God, temptation is something that we all must face. If we fail to deal with temptation, then temptation will deal with us.

The question on my mind is, "When do we face temptation?" Can we define the very moment that it begins? The answer is yes, we can. The Lord does not want us to be surprised, but rather He wants us to be aware of temptation the second it comes into view.

Notice our verse tells us that every man is tempted "WHEN" he is drawn away of his own lust and enticed. The phrase "drawn away" carries the idea of the baiting of a trap. The word "enticed" means "to bait a hook." The word "lust" means "a desire." Let's put this in perspective now. We are tempted at the moment that we desire the bait that has been set before us.

The devil is going to hide the trap and the hook. He only wants us to see the bait. Friend, it's when we start focusing on the bait that we get in trouble. You might think, "How can I overcome the desire?" The way we overcome the desire and defeat the temptation is by focusing on the trap and the hook, and not on the bait. You see, if an animal had enough understanding to know what the trap was, he would bypass the bait. So would a fish if he understood the pain of the hook. It causes you to lose the desire for the bait. If we will look past the temptation and consider the cost and consequences of fulfilling a sinful desire, then there is no temptation. The defining moment is when we detect the lustful desire in our hearts. We must denounce it, turn to God for help, and ask Him to remove it.

"The Deadly Triangle of Sin"

James 1:15 - *"Then when lust hath conceived, it bringeth forth sin: and sin, when it is finished, bringeth forth death."*

The last word in our verse is the word, "death." If you look back through the verse from the word "death," you will notice something rather interesting. Death is the child of sin and the grandchild of lust. Lust gives birth to sin, and sin gives birth to death. Together they form the deadly triangle of sin!

The fourteenth verse revealed that temptation and lust come together. Now, temptation and lust can produce nothing within themselves, but the seed is planted when lust becomes a willful act. You see, the devil cannot make us sin, but he can motivate us to. He can try to bring temptation and lust together in hopes that sin will be born.

The problem with sin is that sin has an end. The end is death! The devil will show you the enjoyment of sin, but not the end. He will show you enjoyment of living a life of drinking but not dying of liver disease. There are many examples of the fun side of sin, but there are just as many examples of the fatal side of sin. Lust, sin, and death weave a deadly triangle that no man can handle.

Our verse says, "Sin, when it is finished." I have seen people live a life of sin, and then one day they said, "I'm through living a life of sin, I think I'll change my ways." You see they were finished with sin, but sin wasn't finished with them. When the time came that they were willing to walk away from sin, they found out that sin had shackled them. It had built a chain, one link at a time. Sin had said, "You may be done with me, but I'm not done with you."

We have all witnessed people who got out of the will of God and turned to sin. Thank God they came back and found forgiveness.

37

However, sin still had a major effect in their life. They went to an early grave because of this deadly triangle. Don't allow lustful desires to lead you down sin's road.

"Do Not Go Astray"

James 1:16 - *"Do not err, my beloved brethren."*

We are encouraged in this verse not to go down the path of deception and compromise. So many around us have changed their doctrine, their convictions, and their principles. They play the role of a victim or a martyr, attacking those who are still holding the line. The reality is that they are convicted by their conscience because they have erred from the truth, and refuse to budge.

I have two important questions on my mind when I consider this thought, "Why did they go astray?" and "How can I keep from following them?" These questions can both be answered by looking back in the fifteenth verse leading up to our verse today.

The reason some have erred is that: 1. They lost their joy (vs.2); 2. Divers temptations (vs.2); 3. A lack of patience (vs.4); 4. A lack of wisdom (vs.5); 5. A lack of faith (vs.6); 6. A double mind (vs.8); 7. Riches (vs.10-11); and 8. Temptation, lust, and sin (vs.13-15).

The reason others have not erred is that: 1. They are true servants of God and the Lord Jesus Christ (vs.1); 2. They have kept their joy (vs.2); 3. Enduring patience in trials (vs.3-4); 4. Seeking God's wisdom, not their own (vs.4); 5. Faith that would not waver (vs.6); 6. A single mind (vs.8); 7. Humility and contentment (vs.9-11); and 8. Endurance against temptation and sin (vs.13-15).

James will turn our attention to the Word of God in the upcoming verses. We know that the Word of God is ultimately what keeps us from erring. The Bible gives us light in a dark world. Purpose in your heart, dear reader, that you are not going to deviate in these last days. Stay with what you know has proven true. Stay with those whom you know are real, and live according to the commandments of the Word of God.

"The Gifts of God"

James 1:17 - *"Every good gift and every perfect gift is from above, and cometh down from the Father of lights, with whom is no variableness, neither shadow of turning."*

Every good gift that we have received in life has come from God. God can only give good gifts, so if what we receive is not good, then it did not come from God. This does not mean that we can always see God's goodness in his gifts, but one day it will be very clear to us.

We should remember that God's gifts are better than Satan's bargains. Satan never gives anyone anything for free. He never gives a gift because he cares; his motive is always to gain and destroy the individual. In fact, instead of calling it a gift, I would call it a trick. That is because his gifts are never as they appear.

Our verse tells us that God's gifts are good, and they are perfect. Think about some of the gifts that you have received from Him: the gifts of health and strength; the gifts of family and friends; the gifts of life and liberty; and the gifts of eternal salvation and eternal security.

Our verse also teaches that there is not the slightest variation in the Lord's gifts. The gifts of God are not just good and perfect, but they are constant. He gives gifts to us every single day. God does not give to us because we are good, but because He is good. Look around you today and see how God has showered you with his gifts.

Remember, we can rest in His gifts. There is no shadow of turning when it comes to God giving us gifts. This means that He will never stop giving to His children. I close with the greatest gift ever given, His Son! Oh, what a gift! Jesus is the perfect gift that keeps on giving to those who receive Him.

"The New Birth"

James 1:18 - *"Of his own will begat he us with the word of truth, that we should be a kind of firstfruits of his creatures."*

Whenever we read this verse we think of the divine nature that is in man. We are "a kind of firstfruits of his creation." When we consider God's creation, the child of God is the highest and most honorable of them all. We have been purchased with the blood of His Son and sealed with His Holy Spirit. We have the divine nature of our Heavenly Father and the promise of eternal life.

Our new birth is a product of the will of God, the Word of God, and the wisdom of God. It is of His own will that he has given us the new birth. He has revealed it to us through His Word. We are both saved and kept by the power of His Word. Finally, the new birth reveals the great wisdom of the Almighty. What wisdom, in that He could take a fallen creature and make Him a new creation. A creation that is greater than it was before. This is the new birth, and the divine nature, that He imparts to the sinner at the moment of salvation.

If you have experienced the new birth, then you should never get over it. You should never be ashamed to share it with others. Tell them how Christ has made you whole. Let the world see that you are not the person that you used to be. Living a Christian life means that we have a higher birth, so we live a higher life. We have been changed from the inside out!

Do you know that you have been saved today? Do you have a new nature? Can you truly say that you have passed from death unto life? Salvation will produce a change in those who possess it. Being born again means you desire the things of God because you possess His nature within your heart.

"The Mature Saint"

James 1:19 - *"Wherefore, my beloved brethren, let every man be swift to hear, slow to speak, slow to wrath:"*

The mature believer possesses several spiritual qualities in his life. Three of those qualities are mentioned here in our verse. I want us to think about the mature believer, and what he displays to others. Ask yourself at the end of this devotional, "Am I a mature saint?" and "Do I possess these qualities in my life?"

First, we see that the mature saint is a good listener. He knows how to take the time to lend an ear to what is being said. This also means that he has great discernment, and he is quick to pick up on what is being said. Now, in context, it is referring to the Word of God. A mature saint has tuned his hearing toward the Word, and he is quick to hear the Lord speaking to him. He has trained his ear on what to hear, and what to tune out. He is good at listening to that which is worth listening to.

Second, we see that a mature saint is a slow responder. He is not quick to give an answer. The mature saint is prayerful and careful with his words. He chooses them wisely, knowing that one day he will give an account to God for what he says. The mature saint realizes that God gave him two ears and one mouth, for the reason that it is more important to listen than to speak. His voice doesn't always have to be heard. An immature saint always has something to say about everything.

Finally, a mature saint controls his temper. This doesn't mean that he does not get angry, but he chooses to get angry about what God is angry about. He has learned to temper the old man and keep him in subjection. Losing our temper is not worth losing our testimony. The mature Christian has allowed the Word of God to sharpen his ear, bridle his tongue and control his temper. Dear reader, may we practice this verse today.

"It Doesn't Work"

James 1:20 - *"For the wrath of man worketh not the righteousness of God."*

The word "wrath" represents the strongest of all passions that a man possesses. It is the highest form of anger. It expresses anger in a natural impulse. The wrath of man can be described as losing his cool and flying off the handle, with no regard for his words or actions, a man so boiling with fury, that he doesn't take the time to think about the consequences of his action or the people he may be hurting around him.

We all know people like the man in our verse. It might be a family member or a supervisor at work. It could be a co-worker, or even worse, someone who attends our church. I do want to note that James is talking to brethren in this verse. The church is the one place where people should not have to see angry people. The world is full of wrath, but the church should be full of love. The church should be a place where people are patient, kind, and gentle.

A supervisor may get his way with employees by displaying wrath. Everyone may walk lightly around that family member who is a hothead. Church members might even avoid that member who claims, "he's short-fused." However, the man full of wrath will get nowhere with God. The Lord will not be moved, or threatened, by a wrathful man.

This verse makes it clear that there is nothing spiritual about displaying wrath. Moses was the meekest man on the earth, but he got angry and smote the rock a second time. His wrath cost him the opportunity to go into the promised land. We should be angry about the things that God is angry about, but our anger should be harnessed by the Word of God. The Lord never blesses the attitude of, "Well, I don't care." We should always care what God thinks about our anger, and what others see when we are angry. God has every right to pour

43

His wrath out on us, but yet He shows us mercy every day. We must display the same character before others.

"The Soil of the Soul"

James 1:21 - *"Wherefore lay apart all filthiness and superfluity of naughtiness, and receive with meekness the engrafted word, which is able to save your souls."*

James sees the heart of man as a garden. If he does not perform maintenance on his heart, it will become overtaken by sin and worldly desires. He must remove the weeds of worldliness and the thorns of wickedness from his soul! He must break up the fallow ground within his heart. A filthy heart is like a garden overtaken by weeds. The heart becomes hard like the ground that has never been prepared.

James is talking to believers about preparing themselves for the Word of God. We are foolish to think we can allow sin to reign in our lives and still receive the Word of God. The phrase "superfluity of naughtiness" means "an exceeding measure of wickedness." D.L. Moody once said, "The Bible will keep you from sin or sin will keep you from the Bible."

Once sin has been removed, our hearts become tender, and our spirits become meek toward God's Word. We do not resist its message nor its demands. After we have received the Word, we enjoy the deliverance it gives us. It saves us from sin and destruction. The Bible keeps us from making the wrong choices if we take the time to receive its instructions.

I challenge you to remove anything and everything that hinders you from growing in the Word. Pull out the weeds of worldliness and the thorns of sinfulness today. Clean out your heart and clear off a place in your schedule to receive what God has for you. Pray for a meek spirit to receive the message. Prepare the soil of your soul for the seed of His Word!

"A Doer or a Deceiver?"

James 1:22 - *"But be ye doers of the word, and not hearers only, deceiving your own selves."*

In this verse, James shares three truths concerning the believer and his Bible. First, he gives us a command to be a doer of the Word. Second, he gives us a warning not to become a hearer only of the Word. Finally, he mentions the danger of deceiving ourselves about the Word.

The Word of God is powerful and can transform our lives. However, we must obey the Word. We must apply the instructions that we read. The Bible is a book of action, and it requires action for those who hear it. The Bible will give us victory over sin, peace in troublesome times, and guidance for our daily living. The key to this kind of victory is obedience!

Those members who only hear the Word but never practice it live in constant defeat and deception. They tell themselves they are okay while they struggle along with no victory. They mark their Bible but do not allow the Bible to mark them. Bible preaching will only fatten the intellect of a hearer but will never develop them into a mature child of God. We must never pride ourselves on how much knowledge of the Word we have gained. We must examine ourselves and ask the hard question, "How much of what I hear do I put into practice?"

The deception in this verse is that believers are fooled into thinking they are spiritual when in reality they are not. They believe they are wise in what they have heard, but they foolishly have not applied the truths. They have built their Christian lives on the sinking sand of how much they've been exposed to rather than the solid foundation of how much they have applied. Ask yourself, dear reader, are you a doer or a deceiver? It's not about how much you have heard, but how much do you obey?

"God's Looking Glass"

James 1:23 - *"For if any be a hearer of the word, and not a doer, he is like unto a man beholding his natural face in a glass:"*

The word "looking glass" is a poetic and archaic way to refer to a mirror, and was considered the proper word to use when referring to one. The word "mirror" was considered vulgar and middle class by the upper class. A mirror is made of metallic or amalgam backing and gives the reflection of whatever or whoever is placed in front of it. The Egyptians made metal mirrors from highly polished copper and bronze as well as precious metals. The oldest known looking glass is over 3,000 years old.

However, there is a looking glass much older than the one dated from modern-day Turkey. James tells us that it's the mirror of God's Word. Like all other mirrors, the Bible tells us exactly what we need to know about ourselves. It reveals our flaws and imperfections. It allows us to see ourselves and correct the mistakes in our lives.

How foolish would it be to walk up to a mirror and see an obvious flaw and do nothing about it? If a person has the ability to correct what they see about themselves, then surely they would not walk away without making those corrections. They would do what was necessary to fix what they see. Yet people hear preaching and read their Bibles and overlook the flaws that they see about themselves. They behold themselves in God's looking glass and then go on their merry way doing nothing about what they have seen.

We all know the importance of looking into a mirror each morning before we show ourselves to others. We are expecting the mirror to reveal the unpleasant things about us, so we can correct them. The same is true about God's looking glass. Have you stopped by it today?

"He Has No Idea"

James 1:24 - *"For he beholdeth himself, and goeth his way, and straightway forgetteth what manner of man he was."*

I want you to imagine a man beginning his morning by standing in front of a mirror. He has showered, shaved, and is now brushing his teeth. As he looks into the mirror, he knows that the next thing on his daily prep list is to apply some hair gel and part his hair in place. He is running a little behind in his schedule today, and in his haste, he forgets to do this part of his routine.

He rushes out the door and is on his way to work. He passes several people on his route, noticing awkward looks and glances as he goes his way. He gets to work and sees folks whispering as he passes them. He cannot imagine why he's getting all of this attention. Perhaps it's the new sports jacket that he purchased over the weekend. It might be the teeth whitener he has been using over the past month. Whatever it is, folks sure are making a fuss about it. He cannot help but feel good about himself.

As the day goes on, his confidence is building about how he has turned so many heads. He strolls down the hallway to use the restroom and to take a glance at this sharply dressed individual. He walks into the men's room, and immediately his confidence is crushed! He looks like he just crawled out of bed! All of a sudden, he remembered that he forgot to brush his hair! He had no idea that he looked so terrible. The mirror told him what he needed to do, but as he got busy, he left the mirror and forgot what he looked like. It wasn't until he came before the mirror again that he saw himself for who he really was. Friend, this is true about many of God's children. If we do not look often in the mirror of God's Word, pride will consume us. We will think we appear to be okay when, in reality, people see us for who we really are. We walk around having no idea how we actually look.

"How to be Blessed"

James 1:25 - *"But whoso looketh into the perfect law of liberty, and continueth therein, he being not a forgetful hearer, but a doer of the work, this man shall be blessed in his deed."*

Every man wants to be blessed in this life. The question is, how do I obtain those blessings? Some go about it the wrong way. Some will do whatever they think is necessary to be blessed. They will lie, cheat, and steal to get ahead in this life. Those who try to be blessed by this method are always disappointed. True blessings can only come from above. The Lord blesses men according to how He sees fit. He blesses some more than others. However, He does not leave us in the dark when it comes to being blessed.

Our verse tells us how a man can be blessed. You see, God desires to bless His children. He wants to be good to us just like we want to be good to our children. God says that if you want to be blessed, then continually look into His Word! After you have looked into it, then live by it. God said if we practice His Word in our daily lives, He will bless our deeds. The question for all of us is, do we want to be blessed by God?

We often think God is hiding His blessings from us or withholding them. Nothing could be further from the truth. The reason some folks are not blessed is that they live a disobedient life. Whenever your children refuse to obey you, then you do not bless them. If they ignore your word, then they miss out on certain privileges. The same is true about our Heavenly Father. If we want to be blessed, then we must take a look in His Word every day and apply His principles for living. They are there because they teach us how to have the best life. The best life is a blessed life and the greatest blessing in this life are spiritual blessings.

"Vain Religion"

James 1:26 - *"If any man among you seem to be religious, and bridleth not his tongue, but deceiveth his own heart, this man's religion is vain."*

Our verse is a simple one to understand. James is teaching us that if our hearts are right, our speech will be right. What's on the inside will eventually come out. A man's religion should be measured both by what we see and what he says. Some are good at talking, but their lives are not separated. They talk a good talk, but they do not walk a good walk. James will deal with that in our next verse.

On the other hand, we must be careful not to deceive ourselves by seeming to be religious. We can learn the formality of religion and deceive ourselves. We have seen this many times in church: people who appear to be spiritual but have a long tongue. They love to gossip and spread rumors. These people cannot be trusted because they tell everything they hear and know. They never care about who they hurt or slander as long as they are the first to tell.

These folks can sing, testify, and preach, but they will have no effect on the cause of Christ. They have grieved the Holy Spirit, hurt their brother, and ruined their testimony. They will only find redemption by using their tongue to repent and confess before the church.

Most members like this in a church have too much pride to do either. Instead, they go on gossiping and slandering with a religion that is as vain as the service they give to God. This verse should cause us all to take inventory of our words and actions. We must guard our speech and put a bridle on our tongue whenever we are around others. We should not waste our words but use them wisely because one day we will give an account of every single word that has rolled off of our tongue.

"Pure Religion"

James 1:27 - *"Pure religion and undefiled before God and the Father is this, To visit the fatherless and widows in their affliction, and to keep himself unspotted from the world."*

After we have viewed ourselves in the mirror of God's Word, we can begin to see others. The Word of God will produce compassion for others who are in need. We will see those who are struggling and in need of our assistance. Pure religion looks for an opportunity to serve both God and man.

Pure religion will put a desire in our hearts to live a godly life. It will create a desire to avoid the world. Whenever James uses the phrase "the world," he is talking about "a society without God." To win the lost, we must keep ourselves clean from the world. Pure religion will produce fruit. It will have a great impact on a filthy world.

The Bible teaches separation. It is one of the first doctrines found in Genesis chapter one. Yet our churches have become defiled by the world. Many churches have opened their doors to worldly philosophies and methods. Somehow, they think this will reach the world if they become a little more like them.

Common sense says that if we are just like them, then why would they want to join us? If what we have is not different from what they have, then there is no need for them to desire God. They will never see their own filthiness if we wallow in the mire with them.

The world will take note of pure religion. They will mark clean living and Bible separation. They may not always accept it, but they will know that we are different. They will see both the compassion it shows and the cleanliness that it produces. This is what they need to see, and this is what we as believers need to reflect. Give me that old-time religion!

James 2

1 My brethren, have not the faith of our Lord Jesus Christ, the Lord of glory, with respect of persons.

2 For if there come unto your assembly a man with a gold ring, in goodly apparel, and there come in also a poor man in vile raiment;

3 And ye have respect to him that weareth the gay clothing, and say unto him, Sit thou here in a good place; and say to the poor, Stand thou there, or sit here under my footstool:

4 Are ye not then partial in yourselves, and are become judges of evil thoughts?

5 Hearken, my beloved brethren, Hath not God chosen the poor of this world rich in faith, and heirs of the kingdom which he hath promised to them that love him?

6 But ye have despised the poor. Do not rich men oppress you, and draw you before the judgment seats?

7 Do not they blaspheme that worthy name by the which ye are called?

8 If ye fulfil the royal law according to the scripture, Thou shalt love thy neighbour as thyself, ye do well:

9 But if ye have respect to persons, ye commit sin, and are convinced of the law as transgressors.

10 For whosoever shall keep the whole law, and yet offend in one point, he is guilty of all.

11 For he that said, Do not commit adultery, said also, Do not kill. Now if thou commit no adultery, yet if thou kill, thou art become a transgressor of the law.

12 So speak ye, and so do, as they that shall be judged by the law of liberty.

13 For he shall have judgment without mercy, that hath shewed no mercy; and mercy rejoiceth against judgment.

14 What doth it profit, my brethren, though a man say he hath faith, and have not works? can faith save him?

15 If a brother or sister be naked, and destitute of daily food,

16 And one of you say unto them, Depart in peace, be ye warmed and filled; notwithstanding ye give them not those things which are needful to the body; what doth it profit?

17 Even so faith, if it hath not works, is dead, being alone.

18 Yea, a man may say, Thou hast faith, and I have works: shew me thy faith without thy works, and I will shew thee my faith by my works.

19 Thou believest that there is one God; thou doest well: the devils also believe, and tremble.

20 But wilt thou know, O vain man, that faith without works is dead?

21 Was not Abraham our father justified by works, when he had offered Isaac his son upon the altar?

22 Seest thou how faith wrought with his works, and by works was faith made perfect?

23 And the scripture was fulfilled which saith, Abraham believed God, and it was imputed unto him for righteousness: and he was called the Friend of God.

24 Ye see then how that by works a man is justified, and not by faith only.

25 Likewise also was not Rahab the harlot justified by works, when she had received the messengers, and had sent them out another way?

"Pyramid Climbers"

James 2:1 - *"My brethren, have not the faith of our Lord Jesus Christ, the Lord of glory, with respect of persons."*

To be like Jesus means we must treat others the way Jesus treated them. He did not elevate personalities, He did not play politics, and He did not show favoritism to those who were rich or prestigious in society. Jesus loved every man and was willing to help those who put their faith in Him. He did not involve Himself in cliques and picks. He made Himself of no reputation and quashed those who were demonstrating respect of persons.

According to James, this has always been an issue in the church. We see this today, as well. Certain members try to climb their way to the "top of the pyramid" in the church, campaigning among the membership to build favor and approval, hoping to gain a place of position or recognition. They form an alliance or a bond that is unhealthy within the church. It can quickly turn into a high school drama team parading around the church, resulting in other members feeling less desirable or unpopular. Those drawn in will help the "ringleader" (or leaders) get what they want. In the end, those same members are left disappointed and deserted by what they thought was a lasting brotherhood or sisterhood that would never end.

How do you keep this from happening to you or your church? First, always prefer your brother before yourself. Second, no personal bond should be so strong that it exceeds your loyalty to the Savior and the leadership in the church. Third, don't be swept away by personality. Fourth, determine not to be intimidated or be a supporter of those trying to develop a following. Fifth, remember Christ is the only One worthy to be at the top of the pyramid. Sixth, if you do make it to the top, you will eventually have a hard fall!

"The Two Visitors"

James 2:2 - *"For if there come unto your assembly a man with a gold ring, in goodly apparel, and there come in also a poor man in vile raiment;"*

James begins an illustration in this verse about two men who visit the assembly. He gives a vivid description of both of these men. As we can see, they are very different in appearance. They are not wearing the same kind of apparel, nor do they have the same status in society. Both of these visitors likely sit in the assemblies of our churches today.

I want us to consider these two visitors, but I want us to think about their souls rather than their outward appearance. Why did they come to church? How do they stand with God? It is more important to be concerned with how they stand with God than how they stand with men.

We cannot assume that one is saved because he is rich, nor that the other is lost because he is poor. The man with a gold ring and goodly apparel could be wretched and poor spiritually on the inside. The poor man with vile raiment could be clothed with humility, robed in the righteousness of Christ, and suited up with the whole armor of God. It is impossible to know the condition of these men merely by how we see them.

I think the lesson here is to focus on the soul of every visitor. Everyone who walks through the doors of your church has a soul. Everyone who attends has a spiritual need. Everyone who attends needs to be preached to and prayed for as if this were their last service. James will deal with partiality in the following verses, but before we get to that point, I want us to think about the great danger of stereotyping people based on what we see. I also want us to consider the great opportunity that can be missed by what we don't see. The next time you are at church and a visitor walks in, see them as God sees them, a soul seeking something from the Father, and a soul that is in spiritual need.

"The Snooty Usher"

James 2:3 - *"and ye have respect to him that weareth the gay clothing, and say unto him, Sit thou here in a good place; and say to the poor, Stand thou there, or sit here under my footstool:"*

It is not the prosperous man wearing the gay clothing, nor is it the poor man wearing the vile raiment that gets my attention in this verse. It is the partial man who is ushering these two men to their seats. This usher seems to be short-sighted and snooty. He is a man who cannot see beyond the superficial. He only sees a man wearing goodly apparel and a gold ring, but he cannot see beyond the temporal things. He never stops to think about how his decision will affect him in eternity.

It is not a sin for a man to be rich, and it is not a shame for a man to be poor. But it is both a shame and sin to treat men unequally like this snooty usher. Christianity places every man on the same level. We have all heard it said, "The ground is level at the foot of the Cross." This statement is true for every sinner, but it is also true for every saint. The only thing special about any man is that God has saved his soul.

We must be careful that we do not elevate people because of their status or success in life. We must also not overlook the blessing of knowing people who are poor by this world's standards but have much more to offer than silver or gold. I also think we should heed the warning to avoid being snooty and mistreating others. The worst testimony is when someone acts like they are better than somebody else. It is disgraceful to lift up some people and put other people down. We must remember that the Lord found us all in the same pit.

"What Right Do We Have?"

James 2:4 - *"Are ye not then partial in yourselves, and are become judges of evil thoughts?"*

Truthfully, nobody wants to be mistreated. Nobody wants to be judged by men, nor do we want them to show partiality toward us. We would not think much of a person who would treat us or our loved ones that way. However, the question we must ask is, "Have I been guilty of showing partiality and prejudging others?"

It is so easy to read these verses and see the sins of others but not ourselves. Pointing out the faults of others never benefits us spiritually. It is a form of judging within itself. Lord, help me not to be any man's judge but to examine myself. It should be our goal to treat others as we would want them to treat us. We should be fair and balanced in all of our dealings.

We have no right to be partial or become judges within ourselves for several reasons. First, because God showed us mercy and accepted us when we were poor and needy, we should exhibit the same grace to all men. Secondly, we should be impartial because the Gospel is a "whosoever will" Gospel. Whether you are rich or poor, the Gospel is for everyone. God loves everybody, and Jesus died on the Cross for everybody. A final reason is that we cannot see the heart of any individual. That is the work of the Almighty and not of those who think they are almighty.

Friend, as long as we strive to treat men the way God has treated us, we will be alright. God will judge them and us as well. He will judge us on how we have treated them. I challenge us all to show unconditional love to those with whom we come in contact. If we show them mercy, then we will find mercy!

"A Tremendous Truth"

James 2:5 - *"Hearken, my beloved brethren, Hath not God chosen the poor of this world rich in faith, and heirs of the kingdom which he hath promised to them that love him?"*

Our verse today can be easily misinterpreted. First, allow me to address what it is not saying. It is not teaching us that God has chosen the poor to be saved and the rich to be lost. Zacchaeus was saved, and Luke 19:2 says he was rich. Salvation has nothing to do with the riches of this world. It is based only on the work of our Savior on the Cross.

You see, a man can be poor in this world and rich in the next world. He can also be poor in this world and poor in the next. The same is true about a rich man. He can be rich in this world and rich in the next, or he can be rich in this world and poor in the next. It proves that neither riches nor poverty has anything to do with salvation.

However, there is a tremendous truth in our text. The Lord has not excluded the poor from His field of service. He is not like the partial usher in this chapter who elevates one man above another man because of his financial status. The Lord has chosen to use men who were poor in this world to show His mighty power! Moses was a poor man whom God used to lead His people out of bondage. The Lord chose David to be King over His people, yet he was a lowly shepherd boy when anointed. Almost all of the apostles came from a poor background.

The truth is that we should never underestimate the poor. God chooses them just like He does the rich in this world. The poor man has a place at God's table alongside the wealthy. Remember, if you are poor in this world, but you are saved, then you will be rich in the next world. Salvation holds riches that are beyond the riches of this world!

"The Church Bully"

James 2:6 - *"But ye have despised the poor. Do not rich men oppress you, and draw you before the judgment seats?"*

A bully is someone we expect to face out in the schoolyard or hallway but never in the church. It's hard to believe that there are bullies in church, but sadly they do exist. James is not going to let the matter rest. There are people in the church who will attempt to buy their way to the top. But, if that doesn't work, they will use bullying as a way to get where they want to be. They don't care who they must step on to gain their desired position.

Many churches are hindered by people who feel that they have ownership over a class, a treasury account, or even the man of God. We cannot allow a church member to bully other members just because they have deep pockets or a lofty position in the church. Having family members buried in the church cemetery for the past seventy-five years does not give them the right to run the church. A spiritual saint is marked by humility and submission.

Church bullies hinder the work of God and discourage the people of God. They oppress the saints with their words and with their actions. They pressure those within the church to do as they say or vote the way they feel. Only those who are loyal to them will be accepted. Church bullies must be reprimanded, which is a big task for the man of God, so he needs the support of the congregation.

The desire is to see them repent and change their ways by knowing their place in the body of Christ. The simple truth is that the only way to defeat bullies is to stand up to them. They will either leave or learn a life lesson that will change their character. James was not afraid to deal with the issue, and we must be the same way.

"It Still Happens Today"

James 2:7 - *"Do not they blaspheme that worthy name by the which ye are called?"*

In the early days of the church, the powerful Sadducees were the ones who were persecuting them. They dragged Christians into court and said false and ungodly things about them and the Lord Jesus. They were blaspheming the name of the Lord Jesus. These religious leaders were using their powerful influence and rich standing to push their own agenda.

Religion has always hated Christianity and elevated man. Christianity reveals man for who he is and allows him to see God as the Supreme Authority. That is why religion despises Christ and loves man. Religion tells man how good he is and how he can better himself by his own self-sufficiency. Religion never does anything for the poor and blasphemes the worthy name of Christ.

What happened back then is still taking place in our world today. We all know the world is a wicked place, but in reality, the world is also a religious place. Religion abounds on all continents and in every culture. No matter where you travel, you will find that man cannot help but worship someone or something. The more religious this world gets, the more wicked it becomes. The more religious it becomes, the more it hates Christianity.

Dear reader, now is the time to rise up and shine. These are the days when our light can burn the brightest! The world can look at us and take note that there is a difference between true salvation and those who blaspheme the worthy Name by which we are called. Take the time to share your faith, but also take the time to show your faith by treating others with love and compassion. Let the world see the love of Christ in you!

"The Royal Law"

James 2:8 - *"If ye fulfil the royal law according to the scripture, Thou shalt love thy neighbour as thyself, ye do well:"*

Laws are passed and put into effect to help us govern our lives. They are for serving the community by helping to provide safety and freedom. It is sad to see the lawlessness that is going on in America today. As Christians, we feel burdened when the wicked rule. They want to ignore the laws that honor God, as well as the laws that uphold decency and morality. They want to pass laws that cause moral decay and bring corruption to our lives.

James tells us that we are to live by an even higher standard than that which society sets. We are to live by the royal law, which was established by a Royal King. Praise God, we are no longer under the law, which our Savior fulfilled on the Cross of Calvary. And He has given us the greatest commandment, which is to love God with all of our hearts!

However, the royal law teaches us to love our neighbor as ourselves. That means that we want those around us to prosper and be blessed more than ourselves. By practicing this law in a world that is so self-driven and self-centered, we will shine brightly as Christians. Sinners will never know the love of Christ until they see it in us.

A good illustration of the royal law would be: after hearing that a car had been stolen out of the parking lot where we work, then walking outside to our parking spot, we began praising the Lord that it was our car that was stolen instead of a co-worker's car. That would be loving our neighbor as ourselves.

"Discrimination Biblically Defined"

James 2:9 - *"but if ye have respect to persons, ye commit sin, and are convinced of the law as transgressors."*

If there has ever been a word misused and abused in our society, it is the word "discrimination." Many use this word to their own advantage, disregarding the damage done to those falsely accused. Business owners have walked lightly for years in fear that an employee would file a lawsuit against their business and take them to court over some trivial act of so-called discrimination.

If I sound a little "put out" with the term, it is because I am, and so are many people in our country. Not that we don't believe it exists, we all know that it does. I do not think that discrimination is confined only to a race of people or a sector of a community. The color of a person's skin or status in society does not matter to me. I have never been in favor of discrimination against any individual. I think that discrimination should be Biblically defined and balanced.

Discrimination is being a respecter of persons. It is a sin to elevate someone because of their financial status or put down someone who is less fortunate. Some of the finest and most intelligent people you will ever meet in life are poor, hard-working people. It is not a sin to be blessed because you work hard and earn benefits. It is not a sin to go to college and earn a degree to obtain a higher-paying job. However, it is a sin to employ an unqualified person ahead of a qualified person because you fear what others may say or do. Friend, that is being a respecter of persons, and that is also discrimination. It is discrimination to punish someone because they are rich and reward someone else because they are poor. Equality means every man has the right to earn his way in life and be treated with respect, regardless of his financial status.

"Lawbreakers"

James 2:10 - *"For whosoever shall keep the whole law, and yet offend in one point, he is guilty of all."*

D. L. Moody gave a great illustration of this verse when he compared God's law to a chain with ten links suspending a man over a precipice. If all ten links were to break, then the man would fall to his death; if only five links broke, he would fall to his death; and if only one link broke, he would still fall to his doom. Regardless of the number of links broken, the unity of the chain is what kept the man from destruction.

James is not saying that if we break one commandment, we might as well break them all. He wants the saints to know whether we break all, or just one, we are lawbreakers, and we are as guilty as everyone else. It puts us all on common ground and reminds us that we are all just sinners saved by grace. We should view ourselves and others this way. It helps us not to magnify our flesh, nor anyone else.

One reason we become disappointed in people is that we build them up in our minds. We think so highly of them and expect so much out of them. When they do not deliver the way we think they should, we feel that they have let us down. We forget that they are also a lawbreaker. Again, this is not a license to do as we please but a reminder that we all fall short of God's standard and glory.

Let us not be so quick to judge, and let us not be so sure to defend. We can be wrong in both directions. Let us be merciful when we need to show mercy and let us take a stand when we need to take a stand. May the Lord help us to consider ourselves when we hear of others who have broken His commands. May we also be reminded that our salvation did not come by keeping the law. Christ was the only man who ever fully kept the law.

"Good Deeds Will Not Do"

James 2:11 - *"For he that said, Do not commit adultery, said also, Do not kill. Now if thou commit no adultery, yet if thou kill, thou art become a transgressor of the law."*

I heard an illustration on the radio by the late, great Bible teacher and radio preacher, Bro. Lehman Strauss, which I thought was interesting. He told of a man in his community arrested for the murder of a girl. He was tried for the murder and found guilty by the jury. During the trial, several witnesses testified of the man's character and all of the good deeds that he had done.

When it came time for sentencing, it was evident that the judge and jury had not been impressed by his good deeds. The prosecution pointed out that the man was not being tried for the laws he had not broken, but for the one that he had. The judge then called the man forward and sentenced him to death in the electric chair.

The man in the story was not guilty of the adultery mentioned in our verse, but he was guilty of murder. Therefore, the final verdict was guilty. He was a transgressor of God's law. For sinners to be saved, they must realize that they are guilty. They must understand that they have transgressed the law of God, which is a difficult task when dealing with a religious but lost person. They cling to their religion and good deeds like a drunkard clings to his bottle. The good deeds of a religious man are as much the Devil's poison as the Devil's brew itself.

Good deeds never have, nor ever will, merit salvation. The guilty can be pardoned only when they realize their state of condemnation. Friend, it is not what you are trusting in to get you to Heaven but Who you are trusting to get you there.

"How Did You Use Your Liberty Today?"

James 2:12 - *"So speak ye, and so do, as they that shall be judged by the law of liberty."*

You would not think that the words "law" and "liberty" would be together in the same context. However, we see both of these words in our verse today. We understand as Christians that we could never keep the law. We know that Christ fulfilled the law. We know that we are not under the law, but we are under grace. We know the Bible is the law of liberty. Most would agree that these are all facts.

There is much controversy today about so-called Christian liberty. My goal is not to dive into that discussion but to point out what James is telling us. You see, we are all transgressors of the law. We have broken the commandments of God, and we are guilty as charged!

Amazingly, the same Book that condemns us also sets us free! The Word of God is the law of liberty! It gives us the freedom to say no to sin, the freedom to serve Christ, and the freedom to worship God and know what His will is for our lives. The Word of God saves us and guides us along our way through life. The same Book that reveals how wicked we are as sinners also tells us about salvation and how to serve and please God in our lives.

James tells us that since we have been set free, we are to live our lives knowing that we will be judged one day by the same Book that brought us out of bondage. We will be judged based on how we used the liberty Christ gave us to serve Him. What did you do with your liberty as a Christian today? Did you waste it on yourself? Is your liberty something you used to justify the worldly and carnal choices you made? Did you use the liberty that Christ gave you to further the kingdom of God and live a life pleasing to Him? How did you use your liberty today?

"A Fair Trial or Free Pardon?"

James 2:13 - *"For he shall have judgment without mercy, that hath shewed no mercy; and mercy rejoiceth against judgment."*

We have often heard people say, "Life is not fair." We all know that God is the Giver of life, so if we say life is not fair, it is the same as saying that God is not fair. Christians believe in the providence of God. We know God is sovereign and providentially works in the affairs of men.

The Lord does not judge based on fairness, but He judges based on mercy. If we got what was fair, then we would receive only judgment for our sins. There would be no pardon, peace, or protection from God. His mercies are new every morning in our lives, and we should rejoice every day that God has extended His mercy toward us. His mercy will cause us to walk humbly before Him and our fellow man. It will develop a character of compassion toward others who are struggling or those who may have done us wrong.

If we demanded a fair trial, then we would be condemned to die and sent to Hell. Instead, we get a free pardon because God is a merciful judge. In return, He expects us to show mercy on others. Find someone to show mercy to today. Be aware of individuals that God places in your pathway. Remember, if we are unmerciful, then God will judge us in the same light. But if we show mercy toward others, then God will bestow mercy on us.

God bestowed the greatest act of mercy toward mankind at the Cross of Calvary. Yet, there was no mercy shown toward our Savior. He did not receive a fair trial, was wrongfully accused, and then crucified. God placed our judgment on His Son so we could have mercy and a free pardon.

"Balancing the Scale"

James 2:14 - *"What doth it profit, my brethren, though a man say he hath faith, and have not works? can faith save him?"*

We have all known people who claimed they believed, but their lives contradicted that claim; there seems to be no fruit of faith in their lives. We have all met this crowd and wondered, "Do they truly know the Savior?"

Just because someone claims to have faith does not mean that they do. James is not teaching us that works are an essential part of salvation. He is simply balancing the scale for us. He is reminding us that faith will produce works. A faith that saves is a faith that works!

I once knew a man who claimed to be a follower of Christ. I would talk with this man and invite him to come to church. He would always tell me that a person could be saved and not be a church member. He would say that you could have faith and not have to live up to a bunch of man-made rules.

I would remind him that what he said was true, but faith will put a desire in your heart to fellowship with other believers. Faith will give you a desire to worship publicly and put a hunger in your heart to hear the preaching of the Word of God. I never did convince the man to come to church, and I never saw one thing in his life that showed evidence of him having true faith. As far as I was concerned, this man was lost. I believe that he had been deceived because his faith profited him nothing. It never produced a desire to please God or do His will.

Dear reader, if you have genuine faith, it will profit you more than all of this world's treasures. It will produce works that will glorify God and bring others to Christ. Works can never produce faith, but they will leave behind a good testimony of the work of faith in your own heart.

"The Poor and Needy"

James 2:15 - *"If a brother or sister be naked, and destitute of daily food,"*

We know that our text today is connected to the context of this chapter. However, I want us to dwell on this verse and consider the poor and needy. As Americans, it is difficult for us to think about people going without the bare necessities of life. Even the homeless in America can find shelter, a soup line, or a local charity to feed and clothe them for free. America is still a land abounding in wealth, allowing even the poor to rise above this verse.

However, this was not true in the day that James lived, and it is also not true worldwide today. In Bible days, some people were naked and starving, and it still happens in our world today. We have all heard the stories of missionaries and seen the pictures of villages and communities that are naked and poor. I remember seeing a picture of a young man who had taken two-liter Coke bottles, flayed them out, tied vines around them, and attached them to his feet to make a pair of shoes. Little children wearing shirts but no bottoms to keep them warm or allow them some dignity. What about the pictures of those whose stomachs have swollen due to the lack of food? Or, the instances where each rib is visible, and their countenance has fallen due to a lack of nutrition? These images break our hearts and serve as a reminder of how good God has been in our lives.

Jesus said the poor would be with us always. The poor need to be clothed and fed, but more importantly, they need the gospel preached to them. Let the brother or sister in our verse today serve to remind us of how good God has been to us. No one reading this devotional has ever had to worry about clothing to wear or food to eat. We must count ourselves blessed, again and again, that God has taken good care of us. We should live every day grateful for the daily provision our Heavenly Father has prepared for us.

"A Worthless Prayer"

James 2:16 - *"and one of you say unto them, Depart in peace, be ye warmed and filled; notwithstanding ye give them not those things which are needful to the body; what doth it profit?"*

We know that prayer is a valuable tool in our Christian life. Prayer opens the windows of Heaven and moves the heart of God. However, there comes a time when we need to quit praying and begin taking action. God spoke about this to Moses in Exodus 14:15 and Joshua in the same manner in Joshua 7:10-11.

God expects us to pray, but then He expects us to act. If we live as if we have no responsibilities other than prayer, our prayers become vain and worthless. Prayer should always be the first thing we do, not our last, and our concern should not end when we say Amen. The prayer of faith will move us to respond. To tell a brother to go in peace and be warmed and filled is a worthless prayer. Neither the man praying nor the man in need has any confidence in this kind of prayer. It is a prayer to ease the conscience of the one who can give but refuses to.

Other examples would be to pray for world missions but never give to world missions; pray for a country that needs the Gospel but refuse to answer the call to preach the Gospel or pray for people in the community to be saved but never knock on their door or pass out a tract. These are admirable prayers, but they become worthless when we are unwilling to do what we know God expects us to do.

We should pay close attention to our prayers. We should ask ourselves, "Am I doing everything God expects me to do concerning this prayer?" If so, you can rest in the assurance that He will do His part. He will be faithful just as He has promised. What about you and me?

"Dead Faith"

James 2:17- *"Even so faith, if it hath not works, is dead, being alone."*

Please note the order in which James is speaking in this verse. He first mentions faith and then works because faith always comes first. Salvation is the result of putting faith in the Word of God and not a result of faith, plus works. That is not what James is teaching. Works can never produce faith, and they are not equal to faith, but true faith will produce works.

James teaches us that when a man puts his faith in Christ, works will follow. These works are not the source of his salvation but evidence that he has faith. When someone says they have faith, but it does not produce works, it is dead faith and only a cheap profession.

Many people today will tell you they believe in God, that Jesus is the Son of God, and that He died on the cross for our sins, but they have never shown any desire for the things of God, and they live in sin and disobedience to God without chastisement. They have no appetite for spiritual things. They have a faith that is dead, and it has gone no further than their intellect. It is simply a head knowledge that has not turned their heart toward God. Therefore, they can sin and feel no conviction because they have a dead faith.

It is hard to understand how someone could look at something that God condemns in His Word and say they see nothing wrong with it, even after being shown in the Bible where it is wrong. They don't feel bad about the way they are living or the things they are doing. They see nothing wrong with it because they are blind. They do not feel bad because their faith is dead, and a dead man feels nothing. How is your faith?

"What Good is Dead Faith?"

James 2:18 - *"Yea, a man may say, Thou hast faith, and I have works: shew me thy faith without thy works, and I will shew thee my faith by my works."*

A lost soul is empty inside with a dark void that this world cannot fill. Once an individual places his faith in the Lord Jesus, that emptiness is no longer there. It is forever gone from their life because faith produces a work on the inside. Immediately, the Holy Spirit moves in and begins to dwell in the new convert's heart. Faith is nurtured by the Spirit and by the Word of God. It will be evident as he grows, and others will see his faith.

Faith produces a desire to seek God, as well as a delight to serve God, and a devotion to share God with others. The spiritual growth on the inside will continue to grow more on the outside. That is God's plan for every one of His children. He wants others to see our good works and glorify the Father.

So, what good is faith that is dead if it produces nothing for the one who claims to possess it or for those whom they meet? Dear reader, we do not have the time to study the faith of those in the Bible, but I challenge you to do so. Examine the faith of Abraham, Isaac, and Jacob. Think about the faith of Rahab, the harlot, Ruth, Esther, David, and Daniel of old. What about the faith of Elijah, and Elisha, and the three Hebrew children? Then go back and read about the faith of Abel, Enoch, and Noah, and then remember the faith of Stephen, Paul, and young Timothy.

Tell me the one thing that their faith has in common. Do you already see it? Do you know what it is? They all had faith in the same Person, and it produced works! It is faith that works! Faith in Christ is not dead but produces! What good is faith that is no good to anyone? How is your faith today? Is it alive or dead? If your faith is dead, I can assure you it has produced nothing. If it is alive, there will be evidence that you can see!

"A Demonic Faith"

James 2:19 - *"Thou believest that there is one God; thou doest well: the devils also believe, and tremble."*

James continues to warn us against dead faith. He wants our faith in Christ to go beyond the intellect. He wants us to have more than a head knowledge; he wants us to have a heart knowledge. Whenever faith is only in the head, it produces lip service but never a change of lifestyle. The individual has no works to follow his proclaimed faith because it is dead, just like he is.

There is another kind of faith James warns us about in this verse. It is a demonic faith that goes beyond the intellect and touches our emotions. It causes a feeling but never takes root in the heart. It is not saving faith, but Satanic faith. You see, even the devils believe and tremble. What they know and believe about Jesus touches their intellect and their emotions but never changes their heart. It never changes their will and desire. The word "devils" is used in the Bible to describe multiple demons. They know who Jesus is and the power that He has. They even become emotionally touched by what they know. It brought fear to them whenever they stood in His presence, yet they rejected Him. They chose to rebel against God and His Son long ago when God cast Satan out of Heaven.

We all know people who have "tried" church. They have an intellectual faith in God. They truly believe He is real. They also have an emotional faith in Him. What they know about Christ stirs their emotions. However, we will see later that they do not have a faith that touches their heart with the desire to surrender their will to Christ! My friend, it takes more than an emotional stirring to be saved. You must choose Christ and surrender your will to Him.

"The Empty Man"

James 2:20 - *"But wilt thou know, O vain man, that faith without works is dead?"*

The word "vain" can be translated as "empty." James has already told us that faith without works is dead. His statement here is more of an interrogation than an exclamation, and he wants the vain man to get it! He wants him to know that there is a void in every man's life that only Christ can fill. Think about this empty or vain man with me for just a moment.

The vain man's words are empty. He is always talking and thinking about the temporary. He dwells on the earthly rather than the eternal. It is hard for a saved person to maintain common ground with a vain man. The reason is that the child of God lives in one realm, while the vain man lives in another.

The vain man's life is empty. He thinks that life is about the riches of this world rather than the glory of the next. He is left empty by the works of the flesh and is more excited about this life than life beyond the grave. He has no assurance or peace in his soul. He may be religious, but he is just as empty as a man who claims no religion at all.

Finally, the vain man's future is empty. He has not prepared for death, judgment, or eternity. All of his works are in vain, and he is still dead in his trespasses and sins. You might be reading this devotional and recognize yourself, realizing that you are this man and need to be saved. If so, then make today your day of salvation.

You may be reading this and know that you are saved but realize that your life is empty or vain. It can happen to a child of God if all you do is work for the Lord, and you never worship the Lord. When we fail to have a personal relationship with the Lord, our works and efforts are vain. That is why our churches are so empty and dead today. Be sure your walk with God is genuine and consistent, and your labor will not be in vain!

"Is Your Isaac on the Altar?"

James 2:21 - *"Was not Abraham our father justified by works, when he had offered Isaac his son upon the altar?"*

When Abraham offered up his son Isaac on the altar, it revealed his faith in God. The offering of Isaac also revealed Abraham's worship, willingness, and witness. Saying goodbye to his father was one thing, but saying goodbye to his son was another. We see several surrenders in the life of Abraham, all of them leading up to this great quest. The offering of Isaac was the ultimate and complete surrender of this great patriarch.

The question for us today is, "Have we placed our Isaac on the altar?" Have we given to God the thing that is most precious to us? Have we given our everything to God? Have we fully surrendered our life to Him and for Him? For Abraham to give his son, he had to be willing to give of himself. The problem in the lives of many saints today is that they are not willing to place themselves on the altar of sacrifice and surrender.

God blessed Abraham for his faith, and He will do the same for you and me. If we are willing to keep nothing and give Him everything without hesitation or delay, then He will open the windows of Heaven and bless us. The reality is that Isaac never really belonged to Abraham anyway. The Lord had given Isaac to him, and He was able to take him from him.

A surrendered saint understands that he has nothing, can do nothing, and can obtain nothing apart from the hand of God. Jesus taught us that we lose our life when we try to find it, and we find it by losing it in Him. Surrender your will to God and place the most precious treasures you have in this world on the altar. God will bless and honor your faith!

"Partners Together"

James 2:22 - *"Seest thou how faith wrought with his works, and by works was faith made perfect?"*

We know that salvation does not come by works. Christ completed our salvation and finished the work at Calvary. However, faith and works are partners together. James teaches this in our verse today. He has been using the life of Abraham to illustrate the great truth of a dynamic faith.

You see, a dead faith produces nothing. It may touch a man's intellect but never moves his heart. Then there is a demonic faith that touches the emotions. We have seen this happen many times in church services. As a man hears the gospel, his intellect is touched, and he knows he's lost and needs Jesus. His emotions are stirred, and he believes enough to tremble just like the devils that James spoke about. The problem is that his will was never changed. He never surrendered to the Lord in salvation, so he goes on as the dead sinner he was before.

Abraham's faith affected his mind, soul, and spirit. His faith touched his intellect, his emotions, and his will. He was willing to obey what the Lord had said to him. Without faith, Abraham could never have done it, and without works, nothing would have been done.

Faith and works partner together. Faith brings us to salvation, and works reveal our salvation to others. If a man says that he has works and no faith, it is certain that his faith is dead. If he says he has faith and no works, his faith is dead as well. We must remember that works can never produce faith, but real faith will always produce works! They are partners together. All the works of Abraham: taking the journey, gathering the wood, climbing the mountain, and placing Isaac on the altar were because of his faith. His works were partners with his faith!

85

"The Friend of God"

James 2:23 - *"And the scripture was fulfilled which saith, Abraham believed God, and it was imputed unto him for righteousness: and he was called the Friend of God."*

The Lord has a lot of children, but He has only a few friends, and Abraham was one of those friends. Exodus 33:11 tells us that Moses was one of His friends. Our verse today takes us back to the covenant that God made with Abraham. He promised that from his seed would come a great nation. Abraham believed God's promise, and it was counted to him for righteousness.

The Lord is a friend that we can trust. Proverbs tells us He will stick closer than a brother. We can go to Him with all of the problems of life, and He is always ready and willing to help us. I like the old song that says, "I'll be a friend to Jesus." Our Savior called us His friend in John 15:13 when he spoke about His death on the cross. We never have to worry about God the Father or God the Son being an unfaithful friend. God is a true friend who loves us at all times.

How can we be the friend of God? We become His friend by getting to know Him more. That means spending time with God regularly. Have a set time to talk to your friend and listen to Him. We can be His friend by sharing our hearts with Him. Tell Him about your struggles and issues in life. Share with Him your burdens and cares as you would a close friend. We become His friend when we rely on His Word as our guide, knowing that He will not fail us or lead us astray. A true friend wants to feel loved, trusted, and appreciated. A true friend wants to feel that you want to be with them because they desire to be with you.

It amazes me that the God of glory would even want to be our friend! Why would He desire our friendship or fellowship? There is only one answer to this question: He loves us! God loves us! Jesus Christ loves us!

"A Faith that Works"

James 2:24 - *"Ye see then how that by works a man is justified, and not by faith only."*

D.L. Moody said, "Every Bible should be bound in shoe leather." This statement had nothing to do with Moody's past as a shoe salesman, but it was about his devotion to the Lord. Like Abraham of old, he was not saved by faith plus works but by faith that worked! Faith will produce obedience in the life of a believer. The works they do will reveal their faith.

I once knew a man who was a drunkard. He beat his wife and children regularly. I can remember as a child being afraid of him. We would go over to his house on the weekends because he was one of my father's drinking buddies. As night came, he became intoxicated, and you could see the anger that alcohol would produce in him. He would boil with fury over the smallest of things.

One day, he stopped by our house and told us how he had gotten saved and quit drinking. He started going to church with his family. He was so sweet to his wife and kind to his children. I never saw that man lose his temper again. Some years later, I was in a church service with him, and he stood and began to testify. I sat in amazement as the tears streamed down his face and fell off his chin. I could not believe how a man who was so full of hatred, anger, and alcohol was now full of joy, peace, and love. No one needed to convince me that he was a new creature in Christ because I could see his faith shining through his works. No one could have changed his heart but the Lord.

Friend, this is what real salvation can do for a man. It can melt the heart of stone and fill it with liquid love for Jesus Christ. It will cause a man to say goodbye to a life of sin and follow a new life serving his Master. It will unlock the chains of sin and set a man's spirit free for all to see!

"She Got Saved"

James 2:25 - *"Likewise also was not Rahab the harlot justified by works, when she had received the messengers, and had sent them out another way?"*

The testimony of Rahab is that she was a harlot. She was called a harlot in the Old Testament and the New Testament. You can read her story in the second and sixth chapters of Joshua. The Hebrew word translated "harlot" in Joshua can also mean "innkeeper," but the Greek word in our text means an immoral woman. She ran a guest house of sin. If this were all there was to tell about this woman, then it would not be worth repeating, but we have some good news about Rahab; SHE GOT SAVED!

How do we know she became a believer? How do we know she trusted Jehovah? We cannot see her heart, and how could we trust the word of such a vile person? I'll tell you how we can know; we see her faith by her works! Her works did not save her, but they testify to us that she had put her faith in the God of Heaven.

Her faith was not an intellectual faith that only produced a head knowledge. Her faith was not an emotional faith that only stirred her emotions but never brought her out of sin. Her faith was a faith that works! It was evident because she was willing to get involved, rescuing others and risking her own life at the expense of the truth. She believed the Word of God that judgment was coming and that she was worthy of death. We find the story of her faith in both the Old Testament and the New Testament.

We never know who might trust the Gospel when we deliver it. It does not matter how hopeless someone appears to be; if they trust the message of salvation, it can change them just like it changed her. We should witness to everyone because the next words we hear could be, "She got saved!"

"Dead Clay"

James 2:26 - "For as the body without the spirit is dead, so faith without works is dead also."

In this verse, James talks about a dead body and a dead belief. They both lack spirit and, therefore, cannot respond because they are dead. The body lacks the spirit of man, and his faith lacks the Spirit of God. All we have of the man in this verse is dead clay.

When someone dies, we make provisions for the best possible burial. We buy a nice casket, clothe them in fine apparel, prepare the body, and make them as presentable as possible. However, there is nothing we can do to change the fact that they are dead. Their spirit is gone, and their body is decaying. The sooner we bury the body, the better.

A man can do a lot to dress himself up spiritually by going to church, singing in the choir, giving in the offering, and serving as needed, yet he will be as dead in sin as he was before he got involved. How many today are holding on to what they are doing instead of what Christ did on the cross? Friend, they lack the Spirit of God, and they are just as dead as a corpse in the funeral home.

When God formed Adam from the ground, he was nothing more than dead clay. He had clay lungs, a clay heart, clay eyes, and clay feet. His entire body was just a body of clay. He had no breath in him because he had no life in him. What made Adam the wonder of God's creation was when God breathed into his body the breath of life! Our physical life came from our Creator. For a man to be born again, he has to have spiritual life. The spiritual life we enjoy came from our Redeemer! This life produces more than a body of clay; it is a faith that works and is alive!

James 3

1 My brethren, be not many masters, knowing that we shall receive the greater condemnation.

2 For in many things we offend all. If any man offend not in word, the same is a perfect man, and able also to bridle the whole body.

3 Behold, we put bits in the horses' mouths, that they may obey us; and we turn about their whole body.

4 Behold also the ships, which though they be so great, and are driven of fierce winds, yet are they turned about with a very small helm, whithersoever the governor listeth.

5 Even so the tongue is a little member, and boasteth great things. Behold, how great a matter a little fire kindleth!

6 And the tongue is a fire, a world of iniquity: so is the tongue among our members, that it defileth the whole body, and setteth on fire the course of nature; and it is set on fire of hell.

7 For every kind of beasts, and of birds, and of serpents, and of things in the sea, is tamed, and hath been tamed of mankind:

8 But the tongue can no man tame; it is an unruly evil, full of deadly poison.

9 Therewith bless we God, even the Father; and therewith curse we men, which are made after the similitude of God.

10 Out of the same mouth proceedeth blessing and cursing. My brethren, these things ought not so to be.

11 Doth a fountain send forth at the same place sweet water and bitter?

12 Can the fig tree, my brethren, bear olive berries? either a vine, figs? so can no fountain both yield salt water and fresh.

13 Who is a wise man and endued with knowledge among you? let him shew out of a good conversation his works with meekness of wisdom.

14 But if ye have bitter envying and strife in your hearts, glory not, and lie not against the truth.

15 This wisdom descendeth not from above, but is earthly, sensual, devilish.

16 For where envying and strife is, there is confusion and every evil work.

17 But the wisdom that is from above is first pure, then peaceable, gentle, and easy to be intreated, full of mercy and good fruits, without partiality, and without hypocrisy.

18 And the fruit of righteousness is sown in peace of them that make peace.

"The Sunday School Teacher" Part 1

James 3:1 - *"My brethren, be not many masters, knowing that we shall receive the greater condemnation."*

The word "master" means "teacher." This word is found fifty-eight times in the New Testament. Jesus was called by this title thirty-one times and used the title Himself eight times. James has a lot to say about the tongue in chapter three. He begins by talking to teachers because they do a great deal of speaking. Teaching is a great responsibility, so we should not be quick to multiply teachers without careful consideration to prayer.

Teaching is one of the speaking gifts mentioned in the fourth chapter of Ephesians. A Sunday School teacher plays a vital role in the church. It is a responsibility to be taken seriously. Teachers will have to give an account for what they have taught in the classroom. The fact that teachers will receive greater condemnation should cause them to bridle their tongue.

A Sunday school teacher should be humble. He should never use the podium to flaunt his ego. We have all heard the teacher who loves hearing himself speak. He talks too much about himself and his personal life and does not spend enough time talking about the text. He is the hero in most of his stories, and he thinks the class is as interested in hearing about his life as he is telling about it.

A Sunday School teacher should be holy. If you are going to teach truth, you should live as an example of that truth every day. We have a lot of disqualified teachers in our churches today. Throughout the week, they live lives filled with worldliness and carnality and then appear spiritual on Sunday. That grieves the Holy Spirit, and their lifestyle is a disappointment to the class.

"The Sunday School Teacher" Part 2

James 3:1 - *"My brethren, be not many masters, knowing that we shall receive the greater condemnation."*

A Sunday School teacher should be honest. If there is anything a teacher should be known for, it should be telling the truth. A teacher should be careful not to embellish or try to "beef up" a story to make it sound better. People should be able to depend on the teacher to stick with the truth of the text. The Bible is not to be used or twisted to say what we want it to say. People should never sit under a teacher that they cannot trust. A teacher should be honest not just in teaching but in their daily lives and business dealings. Who wants to hear a teacher who doesn't tithe or pay their bills?

A Sunday School teacher should be helpful. The attitude of a teacher is vitally important. It is not only what we say but how we say it. It's also the character of the individual when they are away from the podium. Have you ever heard of someone who had the gift to teach but had a poor Christian character? It taints their teaching because we know them on a personal level. On the other hand, we have listened to someone teach whom we greatly respected, and that weighed heavily on their teaching. Their lifestyle made the truths that they taught come alive.

Finally, a Sunday School teacher should be hopeful. A teacher is to be an example and an encouragement to everyone with whom they come in contact. Being a teacher is not just once a week in a classroom, but sharing every day with those around you. Teaching is not a calling; it is a gift that should be taken seriously and never misused or abused with the tongue. I know these truths are right because preaching also includes teaching. A preacher must abide by these same truths and so much the more!

"The Bridle"

James 3:2 - *"For in many things we offend all. If any man offend not in word, the same is a perfect man, and able also to bridle the whole body."*

A bridle is a piece of equipment used to direct a horse. It includes the headstall that holds the bit in the horse's mouth and the reins that attach to the bit. The purpose of the bridle is to restrain the horse when necessary and direct the horse in the right way. It helps to conquer and control the animal.

James teaches that whenever a man controls his words, he is able to have control over his whole body. He is able to control his attitude, his temperament, his thought process, and his actions. Has there ever been a man who never offended in word? James not only knew the man who never offended in word but lived in the same house with this man as they grew up.

James was the half-brother of the Lord Jesus. He saw Jesus on a more personal level than many others would have. Can you imagine living each day with such an example? What a great influence our Lord must have been before His own household. He never spoke an ill word or an unfitting sentence to them. They never saw Jesus lose His temper, and He never had to apologize for verbally abusing or hurting them.

Christ had discipline in His conversation and character, and His Person was utterly flawless. No doubt James was thinking of Him as he penned this verse. You may feel that you could never live up to the standard Jesus has set and that you could never be perfect in your speech and temperament, but dear reader, we all fail just as our brother James did. However, we have a great example, and we must strive daily to choose our words in a way that will not offend those with whom we come in contact.

"The Bit"

James 3:3 - *"Behold, we put bits in the horses' mouths, that they may obey us; and we turn about their whole body."*

The bit is a piece of metal or synthetic material that fits in a horse's mouth and aids in the communication between the horse and the rider. To place pressure in and around the horse's mouth allows the rider to cue the horse when he wants him to stop or change directions, and it reinforces the other control signals the rider may give the horse with his legs or weight distribution.

James reminds us that the bit inside the horse's mouth causes the animal to obey us and allows us to turn their whole body. An average horse weighs 900-2000 pounds, depending on size and breed, and a lean racing-fit thoroughbred weighs between 900-1100 pounds, yet such a small tool controls them.

The illustration simply means that if we, as Christians, will allow the Spirit of God to put a bit in our mouths to control our tongues, then we can bridle our entire bodies. We must do this to keep our bodies in subjection. If we have no control over our tongues, we have no control over many other areas of our lives. Those who say whatever they think will also do whatever they feel like doing because they know no restraints.

The unbridled man with no bit in his mouth is not someone living a free life, but he is living a foolish life. We all have times when we want to have the last word or win the war of words. We should ask ourselves what the trophy or prize is for winning this war. It may be the prideful satisfaction of being able to say that you were right, or maybe it's just the pleasure of living life without a bridle and a bit. We must consider our words because they are a reflection of our character. The words we say to others do not define them as much as they define us.

"The Boat"

James 3:4 - "Behold also the ships, which though they be so great, and are driven of fierce winds, yet are they turned about with a very small helm, whithersoever the governor listeth."

James continues to talk to us about controlling our tongues. In the previous verses, he has given two illustrations concerning the bridle and the bit. He is now using a boat to emphasize this truth. He mentions the size by saying that they can be great vessels. He mentions the struggle as the vessel may face fierce winds when out at sea. He then mentions the steering and how a simple rudder allows the captain to guide it in the desired direction.

The truth of our text is that we all have the opportunity, and responsibility, to control our tongues and guide our vessels in the direction that would be pleasing unto the Lord. We need the Holy Spirit to help us surrender our tongues unto Him and not allow the fierce winds of the world to toss our vessel around. Think about it, what we say with our tongues can lead us in either the right or the wrong direction. We must always be careful in what we say because our words will often determine the outcome of our circumstances.

Dear reader, ask the Lord to stand at the helm of your boat and guide your vessel. Our prayer each day should be, "Lord, I surrender both my words and my will to Thee." Our tongues can be used to guide us and other vessels in the right direction. It is amazing how such a small member of the body can make such a vast difference. "Lord, help me in guiding my tongue today."

"The Boaster"

James 3:5 - *"Even so the tongue is a little member, and boasteth great things. Behold, how great a matter a little fire kindleth!"*

Have you ever met the man in our text? I call him the boaster. I'm not sure if this man has ever done anything of greatness in his life or not, and I'm not sure about his level of skill or ability. It is hard to tell because boasting about everything is what he does best. Some of this man's boasting is true, but his boasting always leads to embellishment. To hear this man talk, he's been everywhere, seen everything, and done everything better than anyone else.

He is his number one fan. He is a legend in his own mind and is constantly impressed with his accomplishments. He loves himself so much that he has no idea how annoying he is to those around him. He loves to hear himself talk, so he assumes that others do as well. He's the kind of guy who doesn't listen to others because he thinks what he has to say is more important than what you have to say. He is impatiently waiting for you to finish so he can tell you something bigger and better.

Whenever he does something or buys something, he makes sure everyone knows about it. His latest purchase is always the best you could buy at the best price. His accomplishment is always the greatest on record. His record, of course, is not factual.

The sad truth is that he cannot see how bad he makes himself look. He allows his tongue to go unfiltered and his ego to go unchecked. He stirs up a spirit of competition among those surrounding him and is a turn-off to those with whom he could have developed a great friendship. Do you know this man, or have you ever met him? Have you ever been him?

"A Fiery Tongue"

James 3:6 - *"And the tongue is a fire, a world of iniquity: so is the tongue among our members, that it defileth the whole body, and setteth on fire the course of nature; and it is set on fire of hell."*

The ancient Greeks considered fire to be one of the major elements in the universe. They placed it alongside water, earth, and air. You can feel and smell fire just like you can feel water, earth, and air. Fire can be extremely helpful to a man if it is used correctly. It can provide him with light and heat. Fire gives us the ability to cook food, forge metal tools, form pottery, harden bricks, and drive power plants.

Fire also kills more people every year than any other force of nature. Fire can become a destructive weapon with almost unlimited power. Just one flame can spread to destroy an entire forest. A small spark on the side of the road can cause vast destruction over hundreds of acres. Whether the problem is accidental or intentional, the results are still the same: complete and devastating destruction that many times cannot be restored or replaced.

James tells us the tongue is a fire! It is not just any fire, but it can be the very fire of hell. He opens and closes this verse with these two truths. Our tongue can be helpful and harmful. It can ignite a flame that could bring total devastation, even resulting in the loss of life. Think about the lives, homes, and churches that have been ruined or destroyed because someone had a fiery tongue. James said it possesses a world of iniquity. There is no end to how much we can sin with our tongue. If the mind can think it, the tongue can say it.

We must be careful that we don't allow our tongues to ignite fires that destroy the lives of those around us. We must guard our

100

tongues and not let them be a tool for Satan to use. Hell has enough weapons without our tongues being one of them.

"A Wild Tongue"

James 3:7 - *"For every kind of beasts, and of birds, and of serpents, and of things in the sea, is tamed, and hath been tamed of mankind:"*

God has given man the ability to tame the wild beast of the field, the fowls of the air, and even the animals of the sea. Animals great and small were placed under the authority of man. If you have ever been to a circus, then you have seen this verse come to light. It is both entertaining and fascinating to watch these animals follow the commands given to them by their trainers.

James uses this illustration to remind us that while man has the capability to tame a wild animal, he cannot tame the tongue. The tongue is every bit as unpredictable as a wild animal. You may have the tongue under control, but it can turn in an instant. The tongue can never be fully tamed, so it can never be fully trusted.

What are we to do with this wild beast? The answer is not to chain it or cage it up. Our tongue is not going to be confined. Try as we may, eventually it will break free of its chain or cage.

I heard a preacher preach years ago on a message entitled "It Will Break Out on You." He talked of a man who was a roofer by trade. He was coming to church and was trying to reform his life by doing better. The man had a foul mouth, and he was attempting to clean up his vocabulary. He was proud because he had gone two weeks without swearing. Then one day while hammering on a roof, he hit his thumb with a hammer. Well, "it broke out on him," and he soon realized that he needed salvation rather than reformation. Dear reader, the only thing to do with this wild beast is to slay it! We must put our tongue on the altar of sacrifice every morning and ask the Lord to set a watch before our mouth.

"An Evil Tongue"

James 3:8 - *"But the tongue can no man tame; it is an unruly evil, full of deadly poison."*

Why is the tongue so evil? Why can it not be tamed? The answer to these questions is simple. The tongue is full of deadly poison. An evil tongue will not just make one sick, but it will destroy the life of an individual. It defiles the man from the inside out. The tongue fertilizes the wicked soil of his soul. The sin of pride, or perversion, that may be lurking in his heart and mind is soon announced by the tongue. The tongue fuels the inward sins by its outward proclamations.

The evil tongue not only poisons the man's soul but also his spirit. I understand that all these sins begin in the mind and heart first. However, I want you to see how the boldness of the tongue feeds the ego and strengthens the sins that are within. It is a deadly poison that not only defiles the individual but also defiles others who drink it.

Think about the deadly poison of a false teacher as he stands before a congregation of people. No doubt, good people are sitting there listening and searching for the truth. Sadly, they drink the deadly poison of false doctrine. The unruly evil of the tongue has spread the deadly poison of false doctrine and has corrupted the souls of those who drank it.

While we can use our tongues to glorify and praise God, we must remember that the tongue is not redeemed. The tongue within itself is anti-God. One day, we will receive a new body, and with that new body, we will have a tongue that will never speak another evil word! The poison will all be gone! It will be a glad day when we never have to worry about saying another evil thing. Our tongue will only speak of the glad tidings of our Savior and His glorious cause. The evil tongue will forever be taken away!

"A Double Tongue"

James 3:9 - *"Therewith bless we God, even the Father; and therewith curse we men, which are made after the similitude of God."*

I remember as a boy, a religious man who lived on our street. I call him religious because I don't know if he was ever truly saved. I'm not saying the man wasn't saved, but I remember questioning his faith in God. I know this sounds judgmental, but the things he said and did were very confusing to me.

I would see him go to church, come home, and even testify about how the Lord had been good to him and his family. I would later hear him curse with my dad and his brothers. He would say things that were not becoming of a Christian. On Sundays, he would speak the language of saints, and throughout the week, he would speak the language of sinners. He would make critical statements about his church and his preacher. It was confusing how a man could bless God one day out of the week and curse man the rest of the week. This man had a double tongue.

Friend, a double tongue is destructive and should not be the testimony of a child of God. How often do we hear people sing "Oh, How I Love Jesus" on Sunday but talk like the world through the rest of the week? A double tongue is the sign of a double-minded man. Let us practice consistency in our speech.

Determine to use your tongue as a tool to minister grace unto those around you. Conversation should be an opportunity to bless the Lord, build up others in the faith, and witness to those who need to hear the good news of salvation. We should never dishonor God or confuse man by having a double tongue.

"A Hypocritical Tongue"

James 3:10 - *"Out of the same mouth proceedeth blessing and cursing. My brethren, these things ought not so to be."*

Our thought in this verse is a continuation of our last verse. James reminds us again not to allow blessing and cursing out of the same mouth. You see, a double tongue is a hypocritical tongue. Our speech can confirm our faith, but it can also condemn our faith. It can reveal any hypocrisy that may be within us.

Some people are good at talking out of both sides of their mouths. What they say is determined by who they are speaking to. They base their speech upon the present conversation. Hypocrites have learned the art of saying the right things at the right time. James says there should be no hypocrisy in our speech, but it should always be the truth seasoned with grace. It should honor God and should be true at all times.

Guidelines and boundaries must be set in place when we are speaking. We must be sensitive to the Holy Spirit and fill our mouths with words that are governed by His Word. Our hearts must be surrendered, and our minds must be saturated with the Book to overcome the hypocritical tongue.

Let us, as Christians, not allow the wrong speech to dominate us. Quickly find an exit whenever the conversation goes down the wrong avenue. Purpose to turn all negative speech toward the upward way. Turn those negative words into words of faith and godliness. Confess any contaminated speech, and make it right with anyone that we may have influenced in the wrong manner. No one has to have a hypocritical tongue. We can repent over it before God and man. We can forsake the hypocrisy and practice a steadfast speech that is pleasant to all those around us.

"The Spring of the Soul"

James 3:11 - *"Doth a fountain send forth at the same place sweet water and bitter?"*

I remember as a boy going with my dad to a spring on the side of the road in the town where we lived. We would take plastic jugs and fill them to the brim with clear, cold water. It tasted very pure and refreshing, especially on a hot summer day. The spring was always faithful to give us the same clear, cold water. Recently, I was driving through my hometown, and I stopped by the spring to see if anything had changed. I took a bottle and filled it up with water from the spring, and after taking a drink, my mind immediately went back to those childhood days. What a blessing to know that after thirty-five years, the spring had not changed.

There was only one kind of water that flowed from that spring, and it was sweet water. You could depend upon the spring to be consistent. Dear reader, how about the spring of your soul? What flows out of your fountain? You see, the fountain represents your mouth, and your mouth reveals what is hidden under the surface.

Whatever is on the inside is going to come out. What flows from us must be as consistent as the spring that I told you about. We cannot allow sweet things to flow from our lips one moment and bitter things the next. No fountain gives both; it is either sweet or bitter. Which is it that flows from you? Does the flow from your mouth offer sweet refreshment or bitter poison? We must allow the Word of God to purify our souls from within.

I've never seen a day when so many people are pouring bitter water on each other. God help us to speak words that nourish and strengthen those who hear them. We must be on constant alert against the bitter waters of this world. We must not allow those waters to become our words. Lord, help us to be consistent, clear, and cheerful in our speech!

"A Simple Fact"

James 3:12 - *"Can the fig tree, my brethren, bear olive berries? either a vine, figs? so can no fountain both yield salt water and fresh."*

James gives us a simple fact that we can all understand. A fountain cannot give forth two kinds of water, and a tree cannot bear two types of fruit. Whenever we drink from a fountain, we expect clear, sweet water. When we plant an apple tree, we expect the tree to produce apples. These are simple facts that everyone would agree on.

The same is true about the vocabulary of the Christian. The listeners expect things that are pleasant to hear. They expect fresh water that replenishes and restores the listener. They expect the right kind of fruit to come out of our mouths. What we say can destroy our testimony if we are not careful. We must choose our words wisely and prayerfully at all times. It is important to ask the Lord for daily guidance regarding our thoughts and tongues.

I challenge each of us to mark our words and do an inventory of our vocabulary. What do we talk about? What kind of words do we use in our reactions and our expressions? How do we affect our listeners? Do we infect our listeners with words and thoughts that are not becoming of a Christian? Does our speech help or hurt the cause of Christ? One final question for us to consider is, are people better off spiritually by listening to what we have to say, or are they hindered spiritually by our words?

Remember, the fruit of a tree has everything to do with the root system. What is inside our hearts will come out of our mouths. That is a simple fact that we cannot deny. You cannot talk out of both sides of your mouth without it telling on you. Dear reader, to find out the condition of your heart, simply listen to your words, and you will know.

"Knowledge vs Wisdom"

James 3:13 - *"Who is a wise man and endued with knowledge among you? let him shew out of a good conversation his works with meekness of wisdom."*

Knowledge enables us to know things in part, but wisdom enables us to put those things together. For example, a man can be a genius, have a photographic memory, master computer skills, and have many intellectual abilities, but he may struggle to complete simple tasks in life. He has knowledge, but he lacks wisdom.

A knowledgeable man may speak many words but never say anything worth hearing. On the other hand, a man with wisdom may have limited knowledge, but he always has something valuable to say. Wisdom comes from God and gives us the ability to apply truth to daily life.

A wise man is known for his words and his lifestyle. James says he shows it out of a good conversation. He does not have to try to impress men with how much he knows or what he says, but he allows his life to speak for him. The Bible tells us that if we lack wisdom, we should ask God for it. He freely gives it to all who will seek His face. That should be the daily prayer of every believer. We need wisdom to live and do the will of God.

The Bible says that "knowledge puffeth up!" Wisdom comes forth out of a meek spirit. Pride is never found in wisdom but is often displayed in knowledge. We have all heard men speak, and while it was clear that they were very knowledgeable, it was also evident that pride had overshadowed their knowledge. Knowledge can be obtained by the work of man, but wisdom is imparted by God. Wisdom will keep a man humble and always reliant on his Father. Wisdom will minister to others and strengthen their spiritual walk. Remember that wisdom is the principal thing in life!

"Self-Promotion" Part 1

James 3:14 - *"But if ye have bitter envying and strife in your hearts, glory not, and lie not against the truth."*

James gives a direct command in this verse to "glory not." The tongue loves to brag on the flesh. We must be careful to guard against lifting ourselves up. The pride of self-promotion has destroyed the testimony of many people. Several years ago, I read a quote that said, "Pride and grace never dwell in the same place."

Some people like to brag about how they have mistreated someone. They think that it makes that person look bad and themselves look good when, in reality, it's quite the opposite. They are glorying in their strife and promoting their flesh. To glory in yourself never brings glory to God. If they claim to be a Christian, they lie against the truth because Christians do not act this way.

Some promote themselves by telling others about all of the good they have done. They don't need the Lord to keep a record of their accomplishments because they already have one of their own. They are quick to blow the trumpet to make others aware of how God has used them. That can also cause envy and strife in the hearts of others because it can make them feel like less of a Christian. Philippians chapter two teaches us to prefer others before ourselves. We should talk about how God uses our fellow brother or sister and not ourselves. Giving God the glory for using others can keep our hearts free from envy and strife.

Self-promotion is like cancer in our society today. Social media has given a platform to any person who desires one, and that has built pride and arrogance in the hearts of many. We cannot put a price tag on humility, and it does not come naturally to any of us. Lord help me not to glory in myself.

"Self-Promotion" Part 2

James 3:15 - *"This wisdom descendeth not from above, but is earthly, sensual, devilish."*

When we promote ourselves, we create envy and strife among others. It will never uplift our brethren or encourage the weak, and glorifying the flesh never glorifies God. When we strive to be the most popular or number one, it is not of God.

Self-promotion is earthly, sensual, and devilish. The Devil's goal was to be number one, and he wanted to promote himself above God's throne. It is so wicked to magnify ourselves! That should be our attitude when it comes to exalting self. We must not be guilty of tearing others down to build ourselves up.

The world was better off without social media. Even though it can be used as a tool, it is often used as a toy. It can also be a weapon to destroy and hurt others. I don't think Jesus would use social media today. I don't think He would be interested in promoting Himself, creating debates and arguments, or name-calling and hurting others. I'm not fussing at you if you have a social media account, but I am saying that the world was better off without it. It has given people boldness, caused strife and envy, and has become more of a weapon for the Devil than it is for God.

Self-promotion has caused us to make celebrities out of singers and preachers. It has built platforms for people that honor men rather than God. It causes us to focus on the earthly instead of the heavenly. One final thought should concern us all; we are like the Devil himself when we promote ourselves. Jesus did just the opposite while on this earth; He made Himself of no reputation. Lord, help us to do the same in this society so that they might see Jesus in us.

"Confusion Baptist Church"

James 3:16 - *"For where envying and strife is, there is confusion and every evil work."*

I want to invite you to Confusion Baptist Church. Allow me to describe the church to you for a moment. Confusion Baptist has the right kind of music, the right Bible, and the right standards. They believe the right doctrine and go out on weekly visitation. This church has many outreach ministries, a great mission program, and the offerings could not be better. The attendance is good, and visitors come on occasion.

However, this church appears to get along on the surface, but it is full of envy and strife. People smile at one another, the choir sings songs with enthusiasm, and the preacher preaches with fervency, but the church is divided. Members talk about one another over a Sunday meal when they go home. Some members even avoid each other altogether, so they don't have to speak or shake hands. The preacher constantly complains about a member and runs them down in front of his family.

Jealousy has filtered into the singing, and the music program has separated some of the singers and musicians. While it appears to be all for the Lord, it's a competition to see who can be the best or most popular. The preacher delivers a good sermon but is self-centered, making much about himself and less about Christ. It appears to be all about the work of God when, in reality, it is full of evil works. You might ask, "Evil works; how is this possible?" Confusion Baptist has become a breeding ground for gossip, hypocrisy, jealousy, lying, envy, strife, malice, and many other works of Satan. The Spirit has been grieved and departed, and Satan is having a field day with the congregation as they play church. What is sad is that it all started with the tongue. The tragedy is that this church breeds confusion, and the probability is that its youth will grow up seeing a congregation and the preacher appearing one way but being another.

"Heavenly Wisdom"

James 3:17 - *"But the wisdom that is from above is first pure, then peaceable, gentle, and easy to be intreated, full of mercy and good fruits, without partiality, and without hypocrisy."*

You cannot put a price tag on the wisdom that God imparts to His children. In one of our devotionals, we discussed the difference between knowledge and wisdom. Wisdom is provided by God, not learned from a book. This verse describes the many characteristics and benefits of wisdom. The things listed in this verse should provoke God's children to seek wisdom.

We never have to question God's wisdom because it is pure. We can always rest in it because it is peaceable. It comes to us gently and guides us when we need it. We can receive the wisdom of God because it is easy to comprehend, even though it is so far above our ways of thinking. It is easy to obtain if we open our hearts to it. The wisdom of God is merciful because He gives it to all who seek it.

God's wisdom bears nothing but good fruit. If we apply it, we will see results that honor Him and are best for us. It is not for a certain few, and it has no respect of persons. It does not matter who you are or where you are from; God desires us to know His will and His way in all that we do.

Finally, God's wisdom is not hypocritical. It will never lead you to be something you are not or do something you shouldn't. His wisdom will be genuine in your soul. It will produce Christian behavior that others can see. Our testimony will shine before all of those around us. Make it your goal to seek His wisdom today!

"The Peacemaker"

James 3:18 - *"And the fruit of righteousness is sown in peace of them that make peace."*

I want to consider those who make peace. The peacemaker is someone who understands the value of unity among the saints. Their goal is to bring people together instead of dividing them. They look for ways to avoid or end any trace of strife that might come up. The peacemaker lives peacefully and enjoys the good things life has to offer. When you practice spreading peace, you can live in peace.

Those who make peace are known by their words. You never have to worry about them creating division within the church. They have a kind, positive spirit. Saints love to be around peacemakers because they build up the brethren instead of tearing them down. The words of a peacemaker can calm others when they are distressed or filled with anxiety. A few encouraging words can change the atmosphere and perspective of others.

The peacemaker is known for their works. They express love in action and are willing to go the extra mile to listen to the needs or complaints of others. They show their desire for peace by attempting to end strife among the brethren. They do not gravitate toward just one group of people in the church. They spread peace through their fellowship and love for all the saints.

Finally, a peacemaker is known for their worship. God blesses those who strive to keep peace in the church by blessing their worship. They receive the full blessings of God in a service because their worship is not hindered by division, jealousy, or a guilty conscience. They are spreading peace, so they live in peace.

James 4

1 From whence come wars and fightings among you? come they not hence, even of your lusts that war in your members?

2 Ye lust, and have not: ye kill, and desire to have, and cannot obtain: ye fight and war, yet ye have not, because ye ask not.

3 Ye ask, and receive not, because ye ask amiss, that ye may consume it upon your lusts.

4 Ye adulterers and adulteresses, know ye not that the friendship of the world is enmity with God? whosoever therefore will be a friend of the world is the enemy of God.

5 Do ye think that the scripture saith in vain, The spirit that dwelleth in us lusteth to envy?

6 But he giveth more grace. Wherefore he saith, God resisteth the proud, but giveth grace unto the humble.

7 Submit yourselves therefore to God. Resist the devil, and he will flee from you.

8 Draw nigh to God, and he will draw nigh to you. Cleanse your hands, ye sinners; and purify your hearts, ye double minded.

9 Be afflicted, and mourn, and weep: let your laughter be turned to mourning, and your joy to heaviness.

10 Humble yourselves in the sight of the Lord, and he shall lift you up.

11 Speak not evil one of another, brethren. He that speaketh evil of his brother, and judgeth his brother, speaketh evil of the law, and judgeth the law: but if thou judge the law, thou art not a doer of the law, but a judge.

12 There is one lawgiver, who is able to save and to destroy: who art thou that judgest another?

13 Go to now, ye that say, To day or to morrow we will go into such a city, and continue there a year, and buy and sell, and get gain:

14 Whereas ye know not what shall be on the morrow. For what is your life? It is even a vapour, that appeareth for a little time, and then vanisheth away.

15 For that ye ought to say, If the Lord will, we shall live, and do this, or that.

16 But now ye rejoice in your boastings: all such rejoicing is evil.

17 Therefore to him that knoweth to do good, and doeth it not, to him it is sin.

"Believer vs Believer"

James 4:1 - *"From whence come wars and fightings among you? come they not hence, even of your lusts that war in your members?"*

James asks two questions in this verse, and he uses the word war in both of them. I think that is interesting because, in the last verse, he used the word peace twice. He expresses how God's people can live either in peace or strife. God wants His children to get along and live in peace rather than strife and envy. Spiritual people desire to have unity.

We must consider the first question in our verse: what is the source of our resistance? Who is behind the wars and fightings that take place among the saints? Anytime a division arises, we should stop and consider the source. I promise that it is not coming from Christ. It is sad when so-called Christian believers fight and go to war against each other. There have been church splits because members fight and argue. Some preachers have parted ways and used the pulpit to attack other preachers with whom they disagreed or disliked. We should not compromise our convictions, but we should not attack other believers. That does nothing to help the cause of Christ.

The other question reveals the answer to the first question. The wars among saints and within saints come from our lustful desires. When we fight with another brother, it's both selfish and Satanic. We're allowing the flesh to dominate and the devil to have control. I know sometimes things happen, and fallouts occur. However, there is a difference between falling out with someone and attacking someone. On a personal note, there is a battle within the heart of every man. His lustful desires are constantly at war with his spiritual desires. Don't allow the spiritual battle between the flesh and the spirit to become a personal battle between you and another brother. Keep your flesh under God's control.

"The Battle Royal"

James 4:2 - "Ye lust, and have not: ye kill, and desire to have, and cannot obtain: ye fight and war, yet ye have not, because ye ask not."

I remember in school that some students just liked to fight. It seemed like they never got along with anyone. They were always trying to start an argument or pick a fight with someone. Those students had as much conflict inside as they created around them. There are people in our churches who are just the same. We all know of people who have been members of more churches than we can count. They have trouble with every pastor and church they attend. Everywhere they go, they get into a fight with someone, and they are always the victim.

Some pastors and evangelists are guilty of doing the same. They rip up churches with their sermons by their arrogance and pride. They feel as if the church owes them something, and they never repent or apologize for how they have treated the people of God. Why is this so? James somewhat dealt with it in our last verse by talking about the war within, but he gives us a little more detail in this verse. He shows us that there is a battle taking place in their lives.

He gives us three reasons for their bad behavior. First, he mentions their *wants* again; they lust, but they do not have. He then speaks of their *ways*. They will stop at nothing to get what they want: killing friendships, destroying a brother or sister, or killing any joy or opportunity someone else might have, so they can obtain. The last thing he mentions is their *war*; make no mistake about it, these people are ready to fight for what they want. Competition is their game, and they will do whatever they can to defeat you. Sadly, if you look at the text again, you will note that they fail each time. James says in every attempt, you have not, cannot obtain, and have not. Friend, the flesh never wins the battle!

"Unanswered Prayers"

James 4:3 - *"Ye ask, and receive not, because ye ask amiss, that ye may consume it upon your lusts."*

The crowd in our text is full of wars, fighting, lust, murder, and in the next verse, accused of spiritual adultery. However, they are people who pray. It is strange how people can be so evil yet still bow their heads and go through the formality of prayer, believing that God will hear them through their selfish pride.

In verse two, he told us that they failed to pray personally, but in this verse, he tells us that they failed to pray properly. People who follow their lustful desires don't pray often, but when they do, their prayers reveal how self-centered they are.

If we are going to have our prayers answered, we must pray according to God's will and not our own. We are to pray in faith, regarding no iniquity in our hearts, and pray in Jesus' name. Examine your heart and your prayer life. Do you pray? If so, then do you pray properly? Prayer is our most powerful weapon if we use it wisely.

Prayer cannot be about us, but it must be about Him. Prayer is our means of communication with God. We have the privilege to pray freely, faithfully, and fervently. We cannot afford to let the flesh rob us of our prayer life. Our flesh will hinder our prayers if we don't crucify it daily.

If you study the prayers of the apostle Paul in the epistles, you find that Paul prayed according to the will of God. That is how he could pray with such confidence and victory in his heart. Putting the flesh in its proper place allowed him to live freely in Christ Jesus. He was winning the war from within and enjoying the victory through prayer.

"Spiritual Adultery"

James 4:4 - *"Ye adulterers and adulteresses, know ye not that the friendship of the world is enmity with God? whosoever therefore will be a friend of the world is the enemy of God."*

The Devil is the number one enemy of God. The world is the number two enemy of God. Believers should feel the same way about making friends with the world as they would about making friends with the Devil. It's strange how many believers today will take a firm stand against Satan while flirting with the world.

God calls this friendship spiritual adultery. We belong to Christ, and He is our Bridegroom. We are to be faithful to Him and not give ourselves to this world. That means we are to reject the world's philosophies, mentality, fashion, and the world's system. Being friends with this world will separate us from friendship with God.

Consider this thought: no parent in their right mind would be friends with a daughter-in-law or son-in-law who was openly cheating on their flesh and blood. They would separate themselves from the adulterer until things were made right. The Father will not be in fellowship with someone who will openly cheat on His Son. Spiritual adultery is just as serious as physical adultery in the eyes of God. There must be a deep devotion to our Savior to have a right relationship with the Father.

Finally, the verse ends with a solemn statement. God makes it very clear that if you are on the world's side, it is the side of the enemy. Dear reader, examine your life to see if you are cheating on God. Have you developed such a friendship with this world that it has separated you from fellowship with the Father? Be sure that you are not on the side of the enemy, but you are on God's side!

"The Flesh"

James 4:5 - *"Do ye think that the scripture saith in vain, The spirit that dwelleth in us lusteth to envy?"*

In the last verse, James places emphasis on the world. In this verse, he emphasizes the flesh. The flesh cannot be tamed, trusted, or tolerated. The Bible teaches us about the depravity of the flesh. James asks a profound question when he says, Do ye think that the scripture saith in vain,...? The answer is, No, never!

The Bible paints a clear picture of the flesh. That does not mean the actual body itself. There is nothing sinful about the body, for God created it. The word "flesh" refers to the old nature and its lust to envy. Our old nature is in a constant struggle with our new nature. The new nature may use the body to bring glory to God, and the old nature may use the body to glorify sin.

We must bring our flesh into subjection and be continually on guard. We must yield it to God daily, nail it to the cross, and let it die. We must be aggressive because it has a spirit of lust and will do whatever it takes to gratify its sinful desires. The flesh is anti-God and wars against everything holy. The flesh does not want to glorify anyone other than itself and will stop at nothing to get what it wants.

I am so glad that we have a Bible to teach us about our flesh. The Bible clearly describes our old nature and teaches us how to overcome the spirit that lusteth to envy. Lord, help us keep our guard up against the flesh at all times.

"More Grace"

James 4:6 - *"But he giveth more grace. Wherefore he saith, God resisteth the proud, but giveth grace unto the humble."*

Our verse today contains three truths about the grace of God. The first truth we see is grace promised. God has not only promised to give us grace but to give us more grace. That means that no matter what we face in this life, God has promised to provide the grace to see us through. As believers, we can rest in the knowledge that this grace will be there to help us in time of need, and that God's grace will never run out! His grace cannot be exhausted, nor can it be extinguished by the affairs of this life.

The second truth in this verse is grace prohibited. God will not give grace to the proud. He will not share His grace with those who choose to trust in themselves. How foolish it is to put our trust in the arm of the flesh. Self-sufficiency has never produced anything but failure. For us to accomplish anything, we must have God's grace to do it. We know that grace and pride can never dwell in the same place. I remember a quote I read a long time ago saying, "Pride is the only disease that makes everyone sick except the person who has it."

The third truth we see is grace provided. The humble receive the grace of God. A man cannot be sinless, perfect, or flawless, but he can be humble. God is willing to work with humble people. He will show them grace every time they seek after it. Even when they stumble and fall, they can find the grace to get back up and carry on. The Lord does not limit His grace toward man, but sometimes man limits the grace of God. He does this by refusing to trust or accept God's grace. Grace is ours for the taking if we will seek it.

"Satan on the Run"

James 4:7 - *"Submit yourselves therefore to God. Resist the devil, and he will flee from you."*

It is never appropriate to brag on the devil. I have heard people testify in church about how the devil had been on their back, yet they said very little about God. God never gets glory when we magnify Satan. However, we must be aware of two things about the enemy. First, we have to remember that he is a defeated foe! God kicked him out of heaven, cursed him in the garden, and then crushed his head at Calvary! One day, He will chain him, put him in a bottomless pit, and finally cast him in the lake of fire. It will be a glorious day to see him meet his final judgment.

The second thing about our enemy is that he never gives up. He may be defeated, but he will still take every opportunity to cause us to stumble. He will do anything in his power to send a soul to hell. If he cannot do this, he will constantly war against the saints, hoping they will fall. He is out to ruin every one of God's children. The question that has been asked by many is this: "How do I overcome the devil?"

The answer to this question is in today's verse. The first thing we must do is submit to God. We all agree that we are no match for the devil in our own strength. Submission to God enables us to face the devil because we do not have to face him alone. The Lord will be our strength when Satan comes to tempt us.

The final thing we must do is resist him. I'm glad we don't have to debate or wrestle with him. All we have to do is say no to his lies and temptations. Friend, if we do not first say yes to God in submission, then we will never say no to the devil when it comes to sin. The good news is that the Lord will fight our battles if we surrender to Him and resist Satan. That will put the devil on the run and help keep us on the right course!

"Draw Me Nearer"

James 4:8 - *"Draw nigh to God, and he will draw nigh to you. Cleanse your hands, ye sinners; and purify your hearts, ye double minded."*

The devil wants us to think that we cannot be close to God. He wants us to believe that it is difficult to have fellowship with Him. The devil is a liar, and we must not listen to his lies. We must trust what God says rather than what Satan tries to put in our minds.

Here we have a clear invitation to draw closer to God. It is such a privilege to fellowship with our Heavenly Father! The invitation comes with a promise that if we draw nigh to Him, He will draw nigh to us. The promise is as wonderful as the invitation itself. What hinders the believer from taking advantage of this invitation? What keeps him from claiming the promise of fellowship? The answer can be one of three things mentioned in our verse. First, it could be dirty hands. Fellowship is broken when a child of God is sinning. You cannot be close to Him and continue doing things that displease Him. Clean your hands of sinful deeds.

The second hindrance could be a dirty heart. Perhaps you have something in your heart that should not be there. Maybe you have an inward struggle that you have not yet yielded to the Lord. You may have unconfessed sin in your heart, and it's grieving the Holy Spirit in your life. We purify our hearts by confessing those hidden sins to God. After confessing those sins, take the time to memorize a verse that will replace the sin that was once there. Hide the Word of God in your heart.

Finally, it could be a double mind. You need to make some decisions and remove the doubt in your life. Quit sitting on the fence. Trust the Lord to help you and allow Him to guide you.

"Real Repentance"

James 4:9 - *"Be afflicted, and mourn, and weep: let your laughter be turned to mourning, and your joy to heaviness."*

The Lord wants our lives to be full of joy and laughter. However, there is a time to mourn and a time to weep. We must weep over sin. There should always be an affliction of the soul when we stray from God. That is what James is telling us in this verse. To experience the joy of the Lord, we must repent of our sins.

When I read this verse, it reminds me of the faces I see in many congregations as I travel to revival meetings. Folks sit silently with sad countenances and look like they have lost their dearest friend. Once the final amen is said, the church is alive with joy and laughter. It seems as if worship is a burden to them. A time that should be joyful has become dreadful in a lot of sanctuaries. Why is this? Could there be a lot of unconfessed sin in our churches today?

To experience revival, we must first deal with ourselves. That means we must deal with any sin that is in our lives. The altar has become nothing more than a decorative piece of furniture in many churches today. We need to get back to preaching and practicing genuine repentance. We must get broken before God.

God responds when His children come clean and honest before Him. Knowing that we see our sin and look to Him for forgiveness gives Him great joy. He is willing to cleanse us from all of our sins and restore our fellowship with Him. Dear reader, I challenge you, as I do myself, to take inventory of your heart and soul. Ask the Lord to show you anything in your heart that does not please Him, then repent with all sincerity before Him.

"The Way Up Is Down"

James 4:10 - *"Humble yourselves in the sight of the Lord, and he shall lift you up."*

We cannot say enough about the subject of humility. It is something that we all must be mindful of daily. God expects us to practice humility in every aspect of life. He wants us to be careful that we don't think highly of ourselves. That is a great temptation in the world we live in today because it is so easy to build a platform for yourself. Many get caught up in self-promotion, and it is acceptable in society. There will always be someone who will agree with you or stroke your ego.

The world doesn't care about a humble man, but the Lord is interested in him. The Lord will elevate the individual who will give Him the glory. As Christians, we must always glorify God for anything and everything we accomplish. Through the years as a pastor, I have observed that the more a person praises the Lord, the more God promotes him. An example of this in the Old Testament would be Joseph. No matter the cost, Joseph honored God, and God honored him.

Jesus is the best example of humility in the New Testament. The Bible teaches that He made Himself of no reputation, but He came as a lowly carpenter's son and lived as a humble servant of God. Philippians chapter two teaches that God exalted Him for His humility. Christ left this example, "with God, the way up is down." Stay humble before God, and He will promote you at the right time and the right way.

Remember, He knows if our humility is true or false. False humility will make a fool out of you and will never fool God. Others may see through your false humility as well. Dear reader, purpose in your heart to keep the correct estimation of yourself and allow the

Lord to use you how He sees fit. Be satisfied to be insignificant, last, or unrecognized by others. Please Him by staying humble.

"Evil Speaking"

James 4:11 - *"Speak not evil one of another, brethren. He that speaketh evil of his brother, and judgeth his brother, speaketh evil of the law, and judgeth the law: but if thou judge the law, thou art not a doer of the law, but a judge."*

James has a lot to say in this epistle about the tongue. He condemns the sins of backbiting, gossiping, and a judgmental attitude. It is shocking that God's children would even need such a rebuke. You would expect the world to bite and devour each other, but never the bride of Christ. The truth of our text is that there are times when the saints speak evil of one another.

Speaking evil of another brother is very detrimental. First, it makes the one speaking look bad. It is wicked to speak evil of a brother who is not present. Whenever you are openly condemning someone, it does not send pleasant thoughts through the mind of the person listening. Even if what you said was true, it doesn't mean that you should tell it. Have you ever thought highly of a believer until you got to know them better, and it became clear that they didn't know how to bridle their tongue? You could not believe what they were saying and immediately lost respect for them as a Christian.

Speaking evil also hurts the one you are judging. Now, I understand the Lord will vindicate the individual if they are guiltless. However, the evil speaking of one brother can poison the mind of another. It could tarnish the character of someone who is not even guilty. People tend to say things, assume things, and draw conclusions without checking the facts. Always remember that there are two sides to every story.

Finally, speaking evil of another brother hurts the cause of Christ and grieves the Holy Spirit. Gossip does nothing to further the kingdom of God. We should practice holding our tongue and building up the brethren, not tearing them down. That is not the principle of compromise but true Christianity.

"Do You Know the Judge?"

James 4:12 - *"There is one lawgiver, who is able to save and to destroy: who art thou that judgest another?"*

We have no right to judge people by our standards because our standards are good for nothing. The standard of man could never measure up to the standard of God. Therefore, we must remember that He is the author and judge of the Bible. God is the lawgiver, and He is the judge of this earth. When we stand before Him, the question that will make the difference is, "Do you know the Judge?" Do you have a personal relationship with Him? Is He your Lord and Master? Is Jesus Christ your Savior?

Our verse clearly states that He is the One who can save and destroy. He has given man life and sent His Son to redeem man's life. He is able to give man eternal life if he will accept His salvation. If man refuses, He will have no choice but to condemn him to the lake of fire one day and destroy his life. The Judgment Seat of Christ is for those who are saved, and the Great White Throne Judgment is for those who will be destroyed.

Dear reader, evaluate your own soul. Are you ready to face God in eternity? We, as believers, must be cautious as to how we judge people. We are to make judgments based upon the Scriptures, but we are not to develop a judgmental attitude toward others. Christians are to show mercy and compassion to those with whom they come in contact. We are to remember the mercy that we received. May God help us to remember that we will all stand before the Judge one day and give an account of ourselves. We are all going to need mercy on that day. Lord, help us reflect the kind of mercy we want the Judge of eternity to bestow on us. Again, I ask you, "Do you know the Judge?"

"The Perfect Plan"

James 4:13 - *"Go to now, ye that say, To day or to morrow we will go into such a city, and continue there a year, and buy and sell, and get gain:"*

When you read this verse, think about the plan being considered. Think with me about a couple planning a trip and deciding to take a journey to a certain city. They have already mapped out the route and made accommodations to live there for a year.

This journey is not a vacation but a business venture to buy and sell. I can imagine the excitement and anticipation of preparing to leave. There are high expectations for a prosperous year. They believe that the sacrifices made will be worth it in the end. They have faith that the benefits will outweigh any struggles they might face.

There is only one problem with what seems to be the perfect plan. The journey includes gain, but it does not include God. They have not said "if the Lord will allow it," but they made plans without considering Him in any way. They were so focused on gain that they forgot God.

How many people make this same mistake today? They have what seems to be a perfect plan for their future, but they have left God out of the equation. They did not seek His direction for their lives or pray to get His approval. Remember, your perfect plan is a plan that will fail if it is not the will of God. We must have His leadership in our lives. The Lord knows what each day holds and whether or not we will even be here. He knows if there is even going to be a tomorrow. For these reasons alone, we must seek His guidance. I don't know what you are planning, but be sure they are His plans for your life!

"What is Your Life?"

James 4:14 - *"whereas ye know not what shall be on the morrow. For what is your life? It is even a vapour, that appeareth for a little time, and then vanisheth away."*

James asks an important question in this verse about life. He wants us to consider life on a personal level. It is a question that every man must ask, and the Bible must answer. What is your life? That is a personal question that demands a Bible answer. Dear friend, you and I cannot properly answer that question alone. I'm so glad the same verse that asks the question also answers it.

First, we see that life is a vapor, which is a chemical composition called H2O-water. Water obeys the downward flow of the world. It follows the gravitation of the valleys and canyons heading toward the sea. A vapor responds to the sun and has its place in the heavenlies. A vapor soars to the highest level, leaving this world. That is the life of a believer! Just like a vapor, our life is heading for the clouds!

Second, we see that life is visible. Human life can be seen and should always be cherished. Life is a gift from God and should never be wasted or misused. Though our days are short on this earth, they can still be significant. We must use every day we have for the glory of God and the good of mankind. Others can be inspired by our lives, because they can visibly see us living for His cause.

Third, we see that life vanishes. Just like the vapor, life is quickly gone. We are here today and gone tomorrow. It doesn't take long to live this life, so we must prepare for eternity and live for Christ. Don't let your life vanish from this world unprepared for the next. Don't waste your life on selfish things and goals that have no eternal value. Lay up treasures in heaven where life matters most.

Live for God and work for eternity, for your life will soon be gone. Ask yourself this most solemn question, "What is YOUR life?"

"Acknowledging the Almighty"

James 4:15 - *"For that ye ought to say, If the Lord will, we shall live, and do this, or that."*

James gives us a great principle to live by every day of our lives. He reminds us to make no plans without acknowledging the Almighty. The sovereignty and will of God should rule our speech and daily decisions. We must exalt the Lord in even the most mundane events of life. Here are a few reasons we should always say, "If the Lord will."

The first reason is that He deserves to be acknowledged. The Lord is worthy of constantly being recognized in our daily activities. He deserves and desires to be in the center of all that goes on in our lives. We can place Him there by simply saying, "If the Lord will."

The second reason is that we do not know what a day may bring. Only the Lord knows if we will accomplish the daily tasks we face. Many people get up with a full schedule, not knowing it will be interrupted. Others never arrived at the intended destination because their lives ended unexpectedly. Dear reader, remember the day may take us by surprise, but it never takes the Lord by surprise.

The third reason to acknowledge the Lord is the testimony it shows to the lost around us. Whenever we say to someone, "I'll be there tomorrow, the Lord willing," it reminds them of the Almighty. A man who may not allow you to witness to him from the Bible may be reached by your acknowledgment of God in daily affairs. It is a simple phrase, yet it can be a powerful witness to a sinner. It may even cause him to pause and ask questions about God that he would have never asked. It is a gentle reminder to those who do not know Him and an encouragement to those who do that nothing can happen in our lives unless God allows it.

"The Wrong Kind of Rejoicing"

James 4:16 - *"But now ye rejoice in your boastings: all such rejoicing is evil."*

James is thinking about those who trust their ability alone to plan their future. The sin in this verse is rejoicing in our own abilities or accomplishments. We often hear and see this in our society today. To place confidence in ourselves is both deceptive and destructive. It reminds me of what the songwriter said when he wrote these words, "The arm of flesh will surely fail you, ye dare not trust your own."

We are to rejoice in what the Lord is able to do, not what we think we can do. We are to glorify God for every good thing that He has allowed us to accomplish in our lives. We are to boast in Him and not ourselves. I think you will agree that no one likes to listen to boasting. An individual who constantly brags about what he has done and what he plans to do is adored only by himself.

If this kind of rejoicing offends us, then think about how it must offend the Lord. He gives man the ability, talent, skill, and strength to do all things. All the Lord wants us to do is give Him the glory due to His name. He wants us to rejoice in Him and not ourselves.

Remember, the wrong kind of rejoicing grieves the Spirit of God in our lives. The wrong kind of rejoicing lifts up the flesh and gives place to the Devil. The wrong kind of rejoicing turns others away and hinders our testimony as a child of God. May we guard our tongues and our spirits by always giving Him praise. May we lift Him up by never making plans without seeking His will and by acknowledging His will in everything we do. Our rejoicing needs to point others to Christ and not to ourselves.

"The Definition of Sin"

James 4:17 - *"Therefore to him that knoweth to do good, and doeth it not, to him it is sin."*

Here we have one of the Bible's definitions of sin. Whenever we think of sin, we often think of doing something wrong. James tells us that sin is also when we know to do good and fail to do it. That is called a sin of omission. Once we have received the light of truth in a matter, God expects us to respond to it. He expects us to apply what we know to our daily lives. To do nothing about it is to sin. How many of us would plead guilty to ignoring the truth of God's Word?

To sin against light is a serious thing. God will hold us accountable based on what we know. Think about how blessed we are in America to have the opportunity to hear preaching and teaching on a regular basis. We have received light that others have never had. The question is, what are we doing with what we know? Are we applying it to our lives?

Whenever the Holy Spirit shows us a truth or impresses on us to do something, we should always obey Him. Our hearts must be surrendered and sensitive to His leadership. But we are to have the same attitude toward the Scriptures. Remember, there is no need for conviction by the Spirit if we have the command in the Scriptures. There is no need to hear a voice if you have a verse. I say this because many today choose not to do good by claiming the Spirit of God has not convicted them. Now, I know He can and that He does convict, but why would He when it's already written in black and white? If we know to do good, we should do it. If we choose not to do the good we know to do, we have sinned. God has given instructions on what to do and how to do it, and it is our responsibility to take what He has given us and put it in shoe leather.

James 5

1 Go to now, ye rich men, weep and howl for your miseries that shall come upon you.

2 Your riches are corrupted, and your garments are motheaten.

3 Your gold and silver is cankered; and the rust of them shall be a witness against you, and shall eat your flesh as it were fire. Ye have heaped treasure together for the last days.

4 Behold, the hire of the labourers who have reaped down your fields, which is of you kept back by fraud, crieth: and the cries of them which have reaped are entered into the ears of the Lord of sabaoth.

5 Ye have lived in pleasure on the earth, and been wanton; ye have nourished your hearts, as in a day of slaughter.

6 Ye have condemned and killed the just; and he doth not resist you.

7 Be patient therefore, brethren, unto the coming of the Lord. Behold, the husbandman waiteth for the precious fruit of the earth, and hath long patience for it, until he receive the early and latter rain.

8 Be ye also patient; stablish your hearts: for the coming of the Lord draweth nigh.

9 Grudge not one against another, brethren, lest ye be condemned: behold, the judge standeth before the door.

10 Take, my brethren, the prophets, who have spoken in the name of the Lord, for an example of suffering affliction, and of patience.

11 Behold, we count them happy which endure. Ye have heard of the patience of Job, and have seen the end of the Lord; that the Lord is very pitiful, and of tender mercy.

12 But above all things, my brethren, swear not, neither by heaven, neither by the earth, neither by any other oath: but let your yea be yea; and your nay, nay; lest ye fall into condemnation.

13 Is any among you afflicted? let him pray. Is any merry? let him sing psalms.

14 Is any sick among you? let him call for the elders of the church; and let them pray over him, anointing him with oil in the name of the Lord:

15 And the prayer of faith shall save the sick, and the Lord shall raise him up; and if he have committed sins, they shall be forgiven him.

16 Confess your faults one to another, and pray one for another, that ye may be healed. The effectual fervent prayer of a righteous man availeth much.

17 Elias was a man subject to like passions as we are, and he prayed earnestly that it might not rain: and it rained not on the earth by the space of three years and six months.

18 And he prayed again, and the heaven gave rain, and the earth brought forth her fruit.

19 Brethren, if any of you do err from the truth, and one convert him;

20 Let him know, that he which converteth the sinner from the error of his way shall save a soul from death, and shall hide a multitude of sins.

"The Tears of Rich Men"

James 5:1 - *"Go to now, ye rich men, weep and howl for your miseries that shall come upon you."*

James is not condemning men for being rich. There have been a lot of rich men used in the work of God. Riches in themselves are not sinful, but men allow riches to corrupt them. Being wealthy can cause men to feel self-sufficient. It can also build pride in a man's heart and make him feel as if he is better than others. Riches can also cause men to be cruel to others, as we have seen in history, paying the poor less to make themselves richer.

The warning is that riches never bring true happiness or real peace, but they can bring misery in life and tears of sorrow. As you read this devotional, there are rich men behind bars who once had everything but still desired more. The desire for more riches compelled them to commit a crime that stripped them of everything and drove them from society, proving that being rich does not give men liberty but can bring them into bondage.

There are rich men living in extravagant homes and driving fancy automobiles, but they have no one with whom to share it. Riches have separated them from their loved ones. They may win the legal battle and gain the family inheritance from their siblings but lose their loved ones for the rest of their lives. Riches brought them nothing but misery.

Tears flow from the rich just as they do from the poor. Rich men cry the same as the poorest of men. Riches cannot dry the tear ducts, but Jesus can! There are riches that money cannot buy. Salvation is a free gift for all men, no matter their financial standing. Riches will surely fail, but Jesus never fails!

"Rusty Gold and Tattered Garments"

James 5:2 - *"Your riches are corrupted, and your garments are motheaten."*

God will not bless someone who tries to gain wealth at the expense of others. Greed has destroyed a lot of men in this world. Some men have gone so far as to sell their souls to the Devil to get rich. Gold fever has brought death and destruction to many good men.

Wealth in itself is not sinful. However, when someone tries to obtain wealth by robbing others, that is a sin. Crooked politicians do it daily in our country. They pass laws to fatten each other's pocketbooks, never caring about the burden they are putting on the American family. God says that their riches are corrupt.

True wealth comes from the hand of God, and we cannot measure it by worldly goods. Those who possess it understand the joy it brings to their soul. We can share the wealth God gives us with the knowledge that He will bless both the gift and the giver.

It is certain that God never blesses a stingy individual, and especially not a thief. At least some of the Scrooges of this world obtained their wealth honestly. There is a curse on those who rob the poor to gain more wealth, that their riches would be corrupt and their clothes would be motheaten!

Think about the Hollywood stars, sports athletes, and successful businessmen of this world who had everything but died with nothing. They spent their days living a crooked life and lost it all in just a moment of a breath. They died in misery with nothing to show for it in this world or in eternity. The truth of the text is that you can't get ahead by stealing from others because God will see to it that you don't. What you gain will rust, and your garments will become full of holes. True wealth comes honestly!

"The Witness of Wealth"

James 5:3 - *"Your gold and silver is cankered; and the rust of them shall be a witness against you, and shall eat your flesh as it were fire. Ye have heaped treasure together for the last days."*

If your wealth had a voice, what would it say? How would it testify on your behalf? Would it testify for you or against you? Now, you might think you are not a wealthy person, and you are barely getting by from day to day, but dear reader, if you compare your possessions to what others have, you will find yourself a wealthy individual. If you have a roof over your head and clothes on your back, you have more than many people in this world.

The people in our text have corrupted wealth. They have obtained it dishonestly. The Lord says that their wealth tells the story of their corruption. It is a witness against them and to all who know them. We have all met wealthy people in this world and heard the story of how they obtained their riches. Some men have gained wealth through inheritance, while others have received it through hard labor and wise investments.

As we start out in life, it is interesting to realize that we spend our health to gain our wealth, then later in life, we spend our wealth trying to regain our health. We spend our time heaping treasures for the last days. Remember, there is nothing wrong with saving for your golden years, as long as your gain is acquired honestly and you retire with a good name. Don't allow your wealth to tell a story that testifies against you. Leave behind a good testimony in this world that will glorify your Heavenly Father and provide a legacy for others to follow.

"The Lord of Sabaoth"

James 5:4 - *"Behold, the hire of the labourers who have reaped down your fields, which is of you kept back by fraud, crieth: and the cries of them which have reaped are entered into the ears of the Lord of sabaoth."*

This title for God is used only here and in Romans 9:29. It is used many times in the Old Testament as the "Lord of Hosts" and is primarily a military term. The Lord is going to return in judgment with His armies one day. He has heard the cries of the mistreated, seen every dirty deal ever plotted, and knows those who have gained their wealth through crooked schemes. He despises the misuse of the poor.

We must remember that things may look unfair in this world, but God has a record book. Not only is there a record book, but there is a reckoning day. He will avenge His children and rescue the poor and needy. He's coming back with His bride to this earth. When He comes, Israel will be delivered, and He will deal with those who have obtained gain by fraud. When the King comes, every crooked path will be made straight!

What a glorious day that will be when there are no more wars! It will be Jubilee for one thousand glorious years upon this earth. King Jesus will sit upon His throne and rule the world with a rod of iron. There will be no mistreatment or wrongful actions taken. The poor will be cared for, and the curse will be lifted. It will be a time like the world has never seen. There will be peace in the valley, the desert will bloom like a rose, and the world will be filled with the knowledge of God. We will all sing of the goodness of the Lord. The Lord of Sabaoth will reign, and we will praise His name through all the land. Dear reader, be sure you are ready for this day to come!

"The Price of Pleasure"

James 5:5 - *"Ye have lived in pleasure on the earth, and been wanton; ye have nourished your hearts, as in a day of slaughter."*

The men in our text have lived in pleasure on this earth. They have enjoyed the luxuries of life by mistreating others. They have nourished their hearts while others have suffered and lived in want. Our verse states that their lives of ease have left them wanting and brought them to judgment. They are like animals feasting their way to the slaughterhouse. They live every day as if they will live forever and have no idea they are heading to the judgment bar of God.

Understand that not all pleasure is sinful. God gave us the things in this world to enjoy. It is the will of God for us to be happy and enjoy the life He has given us. There is nothing spiritual about being miserable in life. Just because we enjoy pleasures does not mean we are living in rebellion. I have met people who thought if you are happy, you are not right with God. I must be the first to testify that I enjoy serving the Lord and take pleasure in the life He has given me here on earth. God did not save us to enslave us.

He also wants us to live according to His plan, not our own. We must be sure that the pleasures we enjoy do not dishonor Him. The wrong kind of earthly pleasures can bring severe consequences to our lives, and in the end, they will leave us wanting. They can bring destruction to our lives and those around us. The Devil will offer a lot of pleasures to turn us away from God's plan for our lives, but we must remember that they all come with a price. Our greatest pleasure in life should be to please our Heavenly Father. I'm reminded of the old song that says, "If it satisfies you, Lord, then it satisfies me."

146

"The Death of the Righteous"

James 5:6 - *"Ye have condemned and killed the just; and he doth not resist you."*

We read in the Scriptures that evil, rich men have killed the righteous. Those righteous heroes of the faith died willingly without any resistance. Think of our Savior who willingly gave His life into the hands of sinful man. Organized religion, money, and power are what motivated men to crucify the most righteous man that ever lived. We know this was all a part of God's plan, but every man involved made a conscious decision in the matter.

I think about men like Stephen, who died at the hand of Saul of Tarsus; James, who died at the hand of Herod; and Paul, who later died at the hand of Nero. Many others are mentioned throughout the Scriptures and church history. Their bravery and Christianity have marked society like no other. The warfare they faced was spiritual, not physical.

Satan used the evil men of this world to falsely condemn and kill the just. Though they went silently to their graves, the voices of the martyrs have continued to ring out loud and clear throughout the ages. The cross cannot be ignored, the church still marches on, and Christianity has spread to the four corners of the earth. The declaration is that God always wins, and the Devil always loses. Righteousness always prevails over unrighteousness.

One day the record is going to be set! One day, every knee will bow before the Judge of this earth. The Lord Jesus Christ will judge the saved and the lost. Those who are in Him will rejoice, and those who have rejected Him will suffer throughout eternity. There will be no escaping the judgment of God when that time comes. The heathen will receive their reward for the wrong they have done in this world. The just will be rewarded for their faithfulness to Him. Those who have given their lives for the cause of Christ will not be forgotten, but they will reign with Him on high!

"Wait for the Rain"

James 5:7 - *"Be patient therefore, brethren, unto the coming of the Lord. Behold, the husbandman waiteth for the precious fruit of the earth, and hath long patience for it, until he receive the early and latter rain."*

The early believers had to live their lives amid difficult circumstances. They faced severe persecution for their faith in Christ. Because their outlook was so dark, James encouraged them with an up look. He reminded them that a better day was coming for the child of God.

The admonishment in this text is to be patient. It is a word James will use repeatedly. In this verse, he gives the believer both a Biblical and biological reason to be patient. The inspiration is that Christ is coming. The illustration is that we cannot hurry the process any more than a farmer can hurry the fruit of his labor.

Life is a process that we all must go through. It requires patience to make it through the difficult seasons of life. However, hope strengthens patience. The farmer has hope because he is waiting for the early and latter rain. The early rain in those Palestinian areas would begin in October after a long dry summer. In extremely dry seasons, it may not even come until November. The latter rain would come in March and continue through April, and then it would be over until October. The early rain would allow him to plant, and the latter would allow him to reap. Child of God, keep plowing and working the field. Keep sowing the good news that Jesus saves. There is a reaping day coming for us all. Be patient and wait for the rain!

"We Are Getting Closer"

James 5:8 - *"Be ye also patient; stablish your hearts: for the coming of the Lord draweth nigh."*

This verse opens with James reminding us to be still. Don't get in a hurry, don't try to get ahead, or worry about the outcomes of life. Just be patient and wait on God. Trust Him even though you may not be able to see or understand what is going on.

Secondly, he reminds us to be strong. We are to establish our hearts. We need strong Christians in this world today, because society is as unstable as water. There are a lot of people living in fear, wondering what is going to happen next. We have a great opportunity as believers to show sinners the strength they can find in knowing Christ.

Thirdly, he tells us to be sure. We can be still and have strength of heart because we can be sure that Jesus is coming. James reminds us of the fact that His coming is drawing nigh. Friend, we are getting closer each passing day to His coming, and we must be faithful until He comes to take us out of this world. Be determined not to give in to the pressures of life and the pleasures of sin in the final stretch of the journey. We are almost at the finish line of this great race.

No matter what we have to face between here and there, make up your mind not to give in. Settle it in your soul that you're not going to give up. Determine that as we get closer to His return, you're not going to coast through your Christian life but press on with fervency for the glory of God.

Remember, every morning the sun rises is one day closer to the coming of Jesus Christ. Today could be the day He comes to catch His bride away. If He comes today, are you ready? Have you made the final preparation?

"The Judge Standeth at the Door"

James 5:9 - *"Grudge not one against another, brethren, lest ye be condemned: behold, the judge standeth before the door."*

I have never understood the purpose behind holding a grudge. I am not saying I am above committing this sin, but it makes no sense to spend our days in bitterness toward another person. It is sad when two brothers in Christ are at odds with each other. We should not allow ourselves to become bitter because of the way others treat us. I would be foolish to think I could live in this world any length of time and not have been mistreated or be guilty of mistreating someone.

What is interesting about this verse is that the condemnation is on the one holding the grudge. When I place this verse in context, I think about how badly the Christians were being treated. The rich had stolen from them and abused them. James writes to encourage them in their trials and afflictions by reminding them that Jesus is coming. Now, he is encouraging them not to spend time holding grudges against those who have done them wrong. If they do, then the condemnation is upon them.

You might wonder how you can let go of a grudge. The answer is in the last phrase of our verse. When we consider the fact that the judge is standing at the door, it will help us overcome our grudges. First, it should motivate us to keep our hearts clean, so we won't have to stand condemned for a bitter spirit. Second, it should help us release our grudges because we know that judgment for wrongdoers is coming soon. That should cause us to pray for those who have done us wrong. Friend, life is too short to spend your days mad and bitter at someone about the past. If you can still replay every detail in your mind, you have not given it to God. Let go of your grudge and live in victory.

"Prophet or Puppet"

James 5:10 - *"Take, my brethren, the prophets, who have spoken in the name of the Lord, for an example of suffering affliction, and of patience."*

The prophets of old are heroes to all of us. We love to hear the Old Testament stories of how the Lord called and used them. Their messages were bold and straightforward. Their visions and miracles left us in awe of the mighty power of God working through ordinary men. No matter how impressed we may be, we must not forget their suffering. The prophets faced great affliction for the message they delivered. God did not raise up prophets to make friends or be popular among the dignitaries. Their ministries were not about luxury and ease. They were not kingdom builders and celebrities like many in the ministry today.

These were men who arose in times of crises or apostasy. They had a message that burned within them. They set out on a mission to deliver the message to the place God had called them. Preaching the burden on their heart was their focus, and then they intended to fade off the scene as they had before. However, many were imprisoned, persecuted, and rejected for what they had preached. These men were prophets, not puppets led by filthy lucre.

Society never praised them or lifted them up. They were never popular or loved by this world for the message they preached. However, things have changed in our day. If we removed salaries, recognition, popularity, and other luxuries, who would continue to proclaim the message in our pulpits today? Ministry has become a means of living for some, but thank God there are still some mighty men of integrity, character, and principle who remain humble, prayerful, ordinary, and not for sale. Society may despise and afflict them, but they are the men standing in the gap and making up the hedge. Man of God, press on!

"The Patience of Job"

James 5:11 - *"Behold, we count them happy which endure. Ye have heard of the patience of Job, and have seen the end of the Lord; that the Lord is very pitiful, and of tender mercy."*

The book of Job contains the conversations between God and Satan, Job and his wife, Job and his so-called friends, and Job with his Creator. The problem with Job's friends is their lack of awareness of the conversation held in the first chapter and their lack of knowledge regarding the blessings that would take place in the final chapter. It's a lesson for all of us that we should be careful and Spirit-led before we administer advice, especially to people going through tough times.

Even though Job was suffering and surrounded by miserable comforters, he still managed to endure. We read of his ups and downs, but I think we can all relate to the struggles he faced within himself. What seems to radiate throughout the book is the patience of Job and the pity of the Lord. God was merciful to Job and used the trials of life to be a tremendous example to others and to bring glory to Himself. He never forsook Job in the worst of times, and He will never leave or forsake us!

The patience of Job through his trials should cause us all to take a step back and look at what we face. I will be the first to admit that I have not been through what Job went through. I have not lost all, buried all, and had more questions than answers. Of course, I have had my share of trials, and we have all seen dark days, but not like this dear servant. We cannot relate to the magnitude of his tests, but we can learn from his example. No matter what we face in our lifetime, we must trust God to see us through it. The patience Job had was the path that led him to his great reward in the final chapter. God blessed him spiritually, physically, and financially because even through his tribulations, he trusted God.

"The Power of Yes and No"

James 5:12 - *"But above all things, my brethren, swear not, neither by heaven, neither by the earth, neither by any other oath: but let your yea be yea; and your nay, nay; lest ye fall into condemnation."*

Our word should be our bond. As Christians, we should be people of integrity. When we give a direct answer to someone, they should be able to take it to the bank. People should be able to trust what we say because we prove ourselves trustworthy. When we answer, there will be no need for earthly oaths and swearing. I'm sure we all remember those childhood oaths we made, such as the promise of "pinky swear," "cross my heart and hope to die," or the ultimate "I swear on my mother's grave." James forbids us from making statements such as these. Our word should be enough when given.

Another reason that he says we should not make these oaths is that we are going to face God in judgment one day. We do not want to fall in condemnation before Him for making such promises. Our conversation needs to be as direct as the Scriptures we read. At least six times in the book of James, he addresses our tongue. The final principle is that if people cannot trust our word, they cannot trust anything about us. It's a reminder that our conversation is in connection with our conduct.

The positive side is that practicing character in our lives and language gives us a powerful testimony. We gain the ears of those who are listening. Think of some precious saint that you admire. Anytime they speak, you are all ears because of the amount of respect you have for them. If they told you something, you would have confidence in them because you know their life. Their "yes and no" carries weight because they have been faithful. They do not need a prop to back up their answer.

"Suffering and Song"

James 5:13 - *"Is any among you afflicted? let him pray. Is any merry? let him sing psalms."*

Is it possible to be afflicted and be merry at the same time? It was for Paul and Silas in the book of Acts. They had been beaten with many stripes and thrown into the inner prison. They suffered affliction for their faithfulness in preaching the Gospel. Even though they were afflicted, they were not through serving God. The Bible says in chapter sixteen that they began praying and singing praises to God. We don't know what they were singing, but it is probable that they were singing psalms. Despite their persecution and imprisonment, they were merry.

I understand that James is talking about two different individuals in our text. However, the principles are simple, when we suffer and have afflictions pray about those physical needs. Then, whenever we are happy, we should sing a song that magnifies the Lord. I'm glad the Christian life is practical and centered around the Bible and common sense. I would tell our girls when they were growing up that if they studied their Bible and exercised their brains, they would always know the will of God. It's just that simple.

However, one of the great mysteries of the Christian life is how God's children can have both suffering and a song. The afflictions of life may rob us of our health, but they do not have to rob us of our song. Singing amid sorrow is something that separates Christians from all others.

You may be reading this devotional and going through great physical pain. You should pray about your affliction and ask the Lord to heal you, and if that is not His will, ask Him to help you as you bear the pain. Ask him to help you keep your song and then share it with others. Practice being merry and being a blessing to those you meet today.

"The Elders of the Church"

James 5:14 - *"Is any sick among you? let him call for the elders of the church; and let them pray over him, anointing him with oil in the name of the Lord:"*

It is a blessing to have a church family. I don't know how a saved person can make it without being part of a local New Testament Church. I know many would criticize that statement, but it is the truth. I joined the church immediately after being saved and baptized, and the Lord has given me the desire to be a part of the church ever since. Some will say, "You don't have to be a member of a church to be saved." That is a true statement, but a saved person will have the desire to be part of a local church.

One reason a church family is important is that there may come a time when you get sick. During that time, it is always good to be connected closely to those who will pray for you. James places emphasis on the elders of the church in this verse. The sick are to call for them to pray over them and anoint them with oil. Thank the Lord for spiritual men in the church who can get a prayer through for others. They are men who walk with God and have proven to be good examples in the church.

We need more men like this in our churches, not only to pray over the sick but also to help strengthen the church in other areas. We must pray for pastors and church leaders today. The devil does all he can to try to discourage and divide them. He knows if he can dismantle the leadership, he can scatter the saints. I encourage you to look around your church and pick out faithful men who help serve the man of God and the membership every week. Pray for those men and encourage them this week. Lift up their hands because there could come a day when you call for those hands to be laid upon you in prayer as you are sick. Thank God for the elders in the church.

"The Prayer of Faith"

James 5:15 - *"And the prayer of faith shall save the sick, and the Lord shall raise him up; and if he have committed sins, they shall be forgiven him."*

James is not giving us a blanket formula for healing the sick. Many believers have fallen sick with a terminal illness and passed away. It was the Father's will for them to leave us, and no prayer was going to heal their body. Prayer is not to accomplish our will but to accomplish the Father's will.

The key phrase in verse fifteen is "if he have committed sins." It would explain why he is calling for the elders of the church. The leaders were in charge of the discipline in the church. Since the individual is too sick to go to church, he calls for the elders to come and pray for him. We read about this kind of sickness in 1 Corinthians 11:30, "For this cause many are weak and sickly among you and many sleep." The next verse in our devotional study will also shed light on this truth. James instructed the early church to confess their faults one to another and pray one for another for healing. It is clear why the individuals were sick, why they were calling for elders, why they were confessing sins, and why they were exercising faith in their prayers.

The principle for us to learn is that sin can bring sickness as a form of judgment. Faith, prayer, and confession can bring healing if we are willing to be open and honest about our sin. I do not want to dismiss the fact that when someone is sick, we should pray for them. All prayers are to be prayed by faith, or the prayers are dead. If you know one who is sick and in need of prayer, pray believing God will heal them. This kind of praying still works today! No matter what report the doctor gives us, we must remember that we are in the hands of the Great Physician!

"The Man of Prayer"

James 5:16 - *"Confess your faults one to another, and pray one for another, that ye may be healed. The effectual fervent prayer of a righteous man availeth much."*

To be right with God, we must confess our sins to Him, but we must also confess our sins to one another. We do not hear a lot of teaching and preaching on that today. We promote testimony services, but what about confession services? If we had more confession services, we would have more testimonial services. I'm not talking about airing out our dirty laundry because there are things that should never be told.

However, let's not use that as a crutch to say we have nothing to confess publicly. The reason that we do not have these services is that it's humiliating to the flesh. We live in a society that likes to promote our good deeds, our accomplishments, our successes, and our blessings. The truth is, no one has ever had a revival or drawn closer to God because of these public announcements. When we humble ourselves, confess our faults, and ask others to forgive us and pray for us, we can see the hand of God moving in our lives.

According to our verse, this man is a humble man, a confessing man, a praying man, and a man of faith. He is a true man of prayer. He keeps a short account with both God and man. He does not play the cover-up or sweep his sin under the rug and act as if it doesn't exist. When he does wrong, he asks God to forgive him. When he has done wrong to others, he confesses and asks the church to forgive him. He is not afraid to confess his faults to others. To have the proper balance, we should never tell people what they don't need to know because this would only serve as a stumbling block to them. Tell them what they already know and what you already know you have done. Be honest with them and yourself before God.

"The Earnest Prayer"

James 5:17 - *"Elias was a man subject to like passions as we are, and he prayed earnestly that it might not rain: and it rained not on the earth by the space of three years and six months."*

Elijah was not a superman, but he was a spiritual man. He was a man who believed in prayer. He prayed believing, he prayed persistently, and he prayed earnestly. That is how we should pray today for our nation and our churches. Earnest prayer is the greatest need of the hour. May the Lord burden our hearts to go deeper in our prayer lives to be more committed and consecrated to Him in prayer. The greatest power in this world is not horsepower or manpower but the power of earnest prayer.

What should drive us to pray earnestly are the results of prayer. Elijah prayed for the impossible, and the Lord granted his request. He shut up the heavens as a result of earnest prayer. He answered Elijah's prayer in a way that left no doubt that God was the One who brought about the answer because it did not rain for three and a half years. This verse proves that God answers prayer. It also proves that prayer can do the impossible. Prayer reveals the power of God. Elijah did the praying, and the Lord did the work!

If you desire the Lord's attention, then earnestly pray. That means to pray believing, with persistence, and pray for the impossible. The same God who worked on Elijah's behalf still works on our behalf. We cannot afford to trust our efforts, but we must look to Him and pray earnestly.

Dear reader, how is your prayer life? Do you earnestly seek Him for the impossible? Remember that your Heavenly Father is only a prayer away. He is waiting for you to invite Him to help you with your needs. He not only wants to work in the realm of possibility but also in the realm of impossibility! Don't just pray but pray earnestly.

"The Second Prayer"

James 5:18 - *"And he prayed again, and the heaven gave rain, and the earth brought forth her fruit."*

The second prayer of Elijah brought about a second miracle. It was amazing to see the Lord shut up the heavens, but an even greater witness to see Him open them up again! The second prayer proved several things to Elijah and those who witnessed the event.

First, it proved that the Lord had not yet finished His work. For three and half years, there had been no rain, and some questioned if it would ever rain again, but the second prayer gave them hope that the Lord was still working. He had not forgotten His people and was still concerned about their situation.

Secondly, it proved that He still answers prayer. I'm sure many people were praying for rain, and when the rain began to fall, it reminded them that God was listening. In dry times we all wonder what God is doing and if He is still listening. The rain proved that the second prayer was as powerful as the first.

Finally, it proved the accomplishment of the will of God. The Lord never does anything without a purpose and a plan. Shutting up the heavens was part of God's plan to get the attention of the King and His own people. It serves a great purpose to all of us as we read the account today.

Don't forget when you pray about things to pray a second prayer. What I mean is, don't assume that the Lord has finished just because He answered the first prayer. Pray another prayer regarding the burden that He placed on your heart. The second prayer may be the greatest of the two. It may also be the most needed prayer.

"A Backslidden Brother"

James 5:19 - *"Brethren, if any of you do err from the truth, and one convert him;"*

James mentions two men in our text. He first speaks of a careless backslider, and then a concerned brother is mentioned. We have witnessed both types of men, and honestly, we have been both. These are certainly two men to whom we can all relate.

Consider the first man in our text. He is a brother who has erred from the truth. He has made a conscious choice to go his own way. He drifted from what once held him in the right way. His decision does not make sense because it does not line up with sound doctrine. We all know someone who resembles this man.

I heard an illustration concerning a man who played an instrument very skillfully. Someone asked him what would happen if he stopped practicing. He replied, "After one day, I would know it. After two days, the conductor would know it. After three days, the orchestra would know it. After that, everybody would know it."

Consider the second man in our text. He is concerned about the path his brother is taking. He realizes that someone must help to convert him from his sinful ways. We must go after lost sinners, but let's not forget those who have strayed from the truth. We need a burden for those who are backslidden and away from God. We must warn them and witness to them as well. They need to see our concern for them and feel our compassion toward them. I hope that if I had ever backslidden, someone would visit me and lovingly warn me of the awful consequences of forsaking the truth. I would not need someone to tell me that the way I was living, and the things I was doing, were okay. I would need a concerned brother to bring me back to the truth.

"A Heart for the Wayward"

James 5:20 - *"Let him know, that he which converteth the sinner from the error of his way shall save a soul from death, and shall hide a multitude of sins."*

The sinner in our text is a believer, not an unbeliever. Sin in the life of a Christian is worse than sin in the life of an unbeliever. We expect unbelievers to sin, but God expects His children to obey His Word, and He will chasten His children whenever they fail to do so.

We should always attempt to win the lost, but we must not forget the brother who has strayed from God. It is easy to talk about those who have fallen into sin, but God wants us to help them. Gossip has never rescued anyone from their sinful path. If we care about our brother, we should pray for him and try to minister to him.

Think about the gain of helping one who has fallen away. That person will experience the forgiveness of sins and deliverance from death. When a brother or sister refuses to get right with God, they are heading for destruction. They will check out of this world early if they do not repent. We must do our part to warn them before it is too late.

Sometimes a believer may think that he has gone too far into sin. He may feel the church would not accept him back, even if he wanted to get right with God. The Devil has a way of convincing some to keep on sinning because they could never be what they once were for God. We must express love and remind the wayward brother that forgiveness is available if he will return. We need to let him see the love of Christ in us as a church family. That does not mean we condone what he is doing, but if he is willing to repent, we will rejoice and be glad. That is what happened when the prodigal son came home in the book of Luke. I challenge everyone to find a wayward believer and carry a burden for him to return to the fold.

Jude

1 Jude, the servant of Jesus Christ, and brother of James, to them that are sanctified by God the Father, and preserved in Jesus Christ, and called:

2 Mercy unto you, and peace, and love, be multiplied.

3 Beloved, when I gave all diligence to write unto you of the common salvation, it was needful for me to write unto you, and exhort you that ye should earnestly contend for the faith which was once delivered unto the saints.

4 For there are certain men crept in unawares, who were before of old ordained to this condemnation, ungodly men, turning the grace of our God into lasciviousness, and denying the only Lord God, and our Lord Jesus Christ.

5 I will therefore put you in remembrance, though ye once knew this, how that the Lord, having saved the people out of the land of Egypt, afterward destroyed them that believed not.

6 And the angels which kept not their first estate, but left their own habitation, he hath reserved in everlasting chains under darkness unto the judgment of the great day.

7 Even as Sodom and Gomorrha, and the cities about them in like manner, giving themselves over to fornication, and going after strange flesh, are set forth for an example, suffering the vengeance of eternal fire.

8 Likewise also these filthy dreamers defile the flesh, despise dominion, and speak evil of dignities.

9 Yet Michael the archangel, when contending with the devil he disputed about the body of Moses, durst not bring against him a railing accusation, but said, The Lord rebuke thee.

10 But these speak evil of those things which they know not: but what they know naturally, as brute beasts, in those things they corrupt themselves.

11 Woe unto them! for they have gone in the way of Cain, and ran greedily after the error of Balaam for reward, and perished in the gainsaying of Core.

12 These are spots in your feasts of charity, when they feast with you, feeding themselves without fear: clouds they are without water, carried about of winds; trees whose fruit withereth, without fruit, twice dead, plucked up by the roots;

13 Raging waves of the sea, foaming out their own shame; wandering stars, to whom is reserved the blackness of darkness for ever.

14 And Enoch also, the seventh from Adam, prophesied of these, saying, Behold, the Lord cometh with ten thousands of his saints,

15 To execute judgment upon all, and to convince all that are ungodly among them of all their ungodly deeds which they have ungodly committed, and of all their hard speeches which ungodly sinners have spoken against him.

16 These are murmurers, complainers, walking after their own lusts; and their mouth speaketh great swelling words, having men's persons in admiration because of advantage.

17 But, beloved, remember ye the words which were spoken before of the apostles of our Lord Jesus Christ;

18 How that they told you there should be mockers in the last time, who should walk after their own ungodly lusts.

19 These be they who separate themselves, sensual, having not the Spirit.

20 But ye, beloved, building up yourselves on your most holy faith, praying in the Holy Ghost,

21 Keep yourselves in the love of God, looking for the mercy of our Lord Jesus Christ unto eternal life.

22 And of some have compassion, making a difference:

23 And others save with fear, pulling them out of the fire; hating even the garment spotted by the flesh.

24 Now unto him that is able to keep you from falling, and to present you faultless before the presence of his glory with exceeding joy,

25 To the only wise God our Saviour, be glory and majesty, dominion and power, both now and ever. Amen.

"Jude, the Brother of James"

Jude 1 - *"Jude, the servant of Jesus Christ, and brother of James, to them that are sanctified by God the Father, and preserved in Jesus Christ, and called:"*

What is the connection between the book of James and the book of Jude? The answer is before us in our text. Jude, the author of this epistle, had a strong connection with James. He was his brother in the flesh and his brother in the family of God. These two brothers were connected spiritually and physically by birth.

Jude was also the half-brother of our Lord Jesus Christ. Jude and James both had a physical and spiritual connection with Jesus. These two brothers in the flesh did not believe in Jesus during His earthly ministry. James was converted after the resurrection (1 Cor. 15:7), as was Jude, possibly at the same time.

Jude reveals his titles in this verse as the servant of Christ and the brother of James. We can see the humility of Jude in these titles. He has no problem being a servant to his Master or preferring his brother above himself. He is not ashamed to be identified with his Savior and his brother. Humility is the key whenever it comes to being used by God. The book of Jude is often overlooked, but it contains a powerful message for the day in which we live.

This book parallels the book of 2 Peter and is the gateway into the book of Revelation. While Peter prophesied that the apostates would come, Jude warns us that they are already on the scene. Dear reader, we are living in the days of apostasy. However, do not be shaken because Jude reminds us in our verse that we are sanctified by the Father and preserved in Jesus Christ, our Savior. Thank God for Jude, the brother of James and the half-brother of Jesus!

"God's Multiplication"

Jude 2 - *"Mercy unto you, and peace, and love, be multiplied."*

What does it mean to be a child of God? According to verse one, we are sanctified, which means set apart. We are also preserved, which means carefully watched and guarded. Finally, we see in verse one that we are called. That means that it was the Godhead that took the initiative in our lives. What a blessing to know that the Father has set us apart, and the Son carefully watches and guards us. It is a blessing to know that salvation began in the heart of God, not in the will of man. We have been called by the Spirit to come to salvation and to serve in His Kingdom. Every man has a will, and every man must make his own choice, but it is God who calls us. That is what it means to be a child of God.

However, that is not all it means! We will all agree that we received more than we expected when we got saved. When most people come to Christ, there is a desire to go to Heaven and miss Hell. While the Lord desires the same, He wants to do so much more than that. He is interested in adding things to our lives from the moment we put our trust in Him.

He doesn't just want to add, but He wants to multiply these things! He adds to our life mercy, peace, and love. His desire is for these three things to increase as we grow in Christ. The mercy of God gives us alleviation, the peace of God gives us assurance, and the love of God gives us affection. We do not serve Him because we have to but because we want to! We serve Him with the knowledge that every day we can find mercy and the peace that passes all understanding, not just given but multiplied! He provides more than we need every day that we live. It is such a blessing to be a child of God!

"Earnestly Contend for the Faith"

Jude 3 - *"Beloved, when I gave all diligence to write unto you of the common salvation, it was needful for me to write unto you, and exhort you that ye should earnestly contend for the faith which was once delivered unto the saints."*

The name Jude means praise. Jude wanted to praise God for the great salvation we have in Christ. But the Spirit of God led him to write about a more pressing matter. It was more needful to write about the battle over the truth. Apostates were rising up, and someone had to call them out before the church. Thank God for preachers who are not afraid to tell the truth. Jude would rather preach a glory sermon than expose the heresy of the day, but a real man of God will always give people what is most needful at the moment because he is in tune with the Spirit.

Jude's purpose for writing was to exhort the saints. He has no intention of being mean-spirited, but he does not want them to fall into deception. An exhortation sermon is not always a lollipop message. Some men think that if they preach a sugar-coated sermon, they are encouraging the saints, but genuine exhortation is to present the truth in a way that admonishes you to contend for the faith. In other words, it challenges you to keep going and live for God.

We need more preaching like this today. We have too much self-promotion and flesh in our pulpits. The average preacher is more about exhibiting himself rather than expounding the Scriptures. That is why our churches are dying, and our pulpits are a joke in many places. We need men who will carry a burden, live holy lives, and preach in power. That is what challenged the church to contend for the faith. We need to get off the sidelines and get on the front line. Let us march toward Zion in these last days!

"The Creepy Old Men of Apostasy"

Jude 4 - *"For there are certain men crept in unawares, who were before of old ordained to this condemnation, ungodly men, turning the grace of our God into lasciviousness, and denying the only Lord God, and our Lord Jesus Christ."*

The phrase "crept in unawares" means "to slip in secretly" or "to get in by the side." These men know how to slide in under the radar. They come in the side door of the church, lurking around to find someone weak in the faith. Jude calls these men out in this verse by highlighting their deception, defilement, deeds, and denial.

These creepy old men of apostasy have been around for a long time. Their goal is to counterfeit, change, and corrupt what is holy. They do this by changing the music, the message, the methods, and the mindset of the church. Apostates don't like words and phrases such as whosoever, fundamentalism, old-fashioned, and King James only, because they define our doctrines, beliefs, convictions, and principles.

These creepy old men of apostasy launch attacks on men of God who, in the past, have won souls, built churches, and witnessed great revivals. Apostates are mockers of old-time religion and those who refuse to abandon the truth. They will say or do anything to gain a crowd.

We cannot afford to be silent in these days. We must not allow the mockers of fundamentalism to silence our mission. Remember, we are the ones who have the truth, and the truth must be upheld. Apostates may flourish, but eventually, they will all fail because there is no substance to their message. Old-time religion has always been under attack by these men, but they come and go while it still remains! After being saved for thirty-five years, I'm still happy to say that I know the truth, and that I grew up in the "Old-time way!"

"You Already Know This"

Jude 5 - *"I will therefore put you in remembrance, though ye once knew this, how that the Lord, having saved the people out of the land of Egypt, afterward destroyed them that believed not."*

Jude reminds us of something that we already know. We can read in the Old Testament how God brought His people out of Egypt and saved them from a life of bondage. You would think that no one would ever forget the miracle of the crossing of the Red Sea. How could anyone ever live in unbelief after seeing the power of God on that day? All the Israelites that crossed over witnessed God's deliverance, but not all trusted in His deliverance. That is how apostasy begins in the heart of an individual. They reject the light and choose not to believe.

There are those who do not believe because they have never heard or seen the mighty works of God. However, there are others who have chosen to reject the things that they have heard and seen. They deny the truth of God and turn it into a lie. To discard the light of God's Word is a serious thing. It's one thing to sin without knowledge, but to sin against the Word can bring swift destruction.

Jude is teaching us in this verse that privilege brings responsibility, and God cannot overlook the sins of His people. Anyone who chooses to walk in unbelief or follow false teachings will end up in destruction, because unbelief leads to corruption. When a person chooses not to believe the truth, the only thing left is to believe a lie. Jude has given us the first of three Old Testament examples of apostasy. He is reminding us of their corruption and their destruction. In a world full of lies and deceit, I'm thankful that I know the truth, and I'm grateful that I have a solid foundation to stand on.

"The Imprisonment of Angels"

Jude 6 - *"And the angels which kept not their first estate, but left their own habitation, he hath reserved in everlasting chains under darkness unto the judgment of the great day."*

Many believe that the history of these angels on earth is in Genesis 6, where they cohabited with women. The word for "habitation" means a dwelling place. These angels fell not once but twice. They fell for the first time with Lucifer from Heaven. They fell a second time when they went lusting after strange flesh. They are no longer free to roam the earth like other demons but apprehended by God until the great day of judgment and reserved in chains due to their apostasy.

Apostasy always leads to chains and imprisonment. The world would have us believe that rejecting God's Word and choosing our own way leads to a life of freedom. That is nothing more than a lie of the devil. Look at these angels and see where rejecting God's light and doing their own thing has brought them. They are living in the worst prison of all! Chasing strange flesh has placed them in the lowest part of Hell, waiting for God's final judgment, the Lake of Fire.

Can you imagine going from the glories of Heaven and singing the praises of God to the darkest part of the underworld to be chained and tormented until the final day of judgment? These angels are examples of how far apostasy can lead someone and how terrible the bondage can become.

The imprisonment of these angels also reminds us that God has not forgotten those who reject and rebel against truth. A day of judgment is coming for every apostate. Our God will have the final say! He will punish those who have corrupted others and led them astray.

"Strange Flesh"

Jude 7 - *"Even as Sodom and Gomorrha, and the cities about them in like manner, giving themselves over to fornication, and going after strange flesh, are set forth for an example, suffering the vengeance of eternal fire."*

The ungodly living in Sodom and Gomorrah has often been the pattern for apostates. These unholy cities were rampant with false teaching, corruption, and perverted lifestyles. They relished in vile, wicked activities and praised those going after strange flesh. The Lord made a historical example out of these ungodly cities. He buried both of them in the depths of the Dead Sea. He made it clear that He does not accept the perverted lifestyle of sodomy. God will never put His blessing on those who go after strange flesh.

It saddens me whenever I think about the condition of our nation today and how far we have drifted from God, leaving the moral principles of His Word and embracing the sins of Sodom and Gomorrah. The crooked and corrupt politicians of our day have given in to the bribes and political pressures of society. They have legalized same-sex marriages and allowed them to adopt children. They will give an account to God for this wickedness one day.

Sodomites parade in our streets, teach in our public schools, work in our government buildings, and now participate in so-called worship services in local churches. These are the signs of a nation that has turned its back on God and embraced the apostates of our day. They have rejected morality and followed after strange flesh. America is living the same way as Sodom and Gomorrah and will reap the same results as these cities. God is bringing swift judgment upon our nation today because of its perversion. As Christians, we must shine our lights and pray that, in wrath, He will remember mercy.

"Filthy Dreamers"

Jude 8 - *"Likewise also these filthy dreamers defile the flesh, despise dominion, and speak evil of dignities."*

The morals of our nation have been decaying for decades. America has long accepted sins such as fornication, adultery, divorce, and pornography. Hollywood has not only whitewashed these sins but has strongly advocated them within the movie industry. The slogan "sex sells" is their theme, and family values are destroyed by these filthy dreamers.

They are now taking their perversion to an even darker and more depraved level by promoting the LGBT movement. They want to exalt their wickedness and shame anyone who stands against it. They are trying to force it on our children and promote it in their movies, magazines, and music. Our public-school systems are no longer about education but have become about indoctrination.

However, the shocking reality is that these filthy dreamers did not start in Hollywood; they began in the church. They did not start out wearing the title of a politician but rather the title of a preacher. This country became derailed when people started rejecting the truth of God's Word. This nation started down this slippery slope when we allowed these filthy dreamers to invade our colleges and churches with their corrupt bibles and beliefs. People began turning their ears away from the truth and traded the power of God for a form of godliness. Now, look where we are today. Apostasy has filled our land, truth has fallen in the streets, and they are teaching our children that they can be a boy, a girl, or even an animal if they want to. We need old-time preaching of the Bible now more than ever! May the Lord give us another generation of men who will cry aloud and spare not about the sins of our nation.

"Facing the Devil"

Jude 9 - *"Yet Michael the archangel, when contending with the devil he disputed about the body of Moses, durst not bring against him a railing accusation, but said, The Lord rebuke thee."*

Our verse reminds us of the rank, the responsibility, and the restraint of Michael, the archangel, when dealing with the Devil. Even though Michael is the chief angel with great power and ability, he leaves the judgment of Satan up to the Lord and not himself. It is unknown how often any of us actually face the Devil. We undoubtedly battle our flesh and the world more than him personally, but there are some things we should remember when we do encounter him.

First, we must realize that we are no match for him. The Charismatic Movement teaches that we should command Satan and that we have power in the name of Jesus. I certainly believe that we have power in the name of Jesus, but that does not mean we have the right or the authority to start commanding the Devil. When fighting him, we are to seek God's help and use the Sword of the Spirit, which is the Word of God. It will be what God has said that will defeat him and not what we have said. We must remember that we are no match for him because we are just flesh. Michael left the battle to the Lord, which is what we should do.

Another thing to remember when facing the Devil is that we should not give him any glory. We should never brag about him or credit him for the hard times he has given us. He wants us to sing his praise for troubling our lives, but we should magnify God in our troubled times. That is what will defeat the Devil and strengthen our faith. When, and if, we face Satan, may we be like Michael by walking lightly and leaving the real battle up to God.

181

"Brute Beasts"

Jude 10 - *"But these speak evil of those things which they know not: but what they know naturally, as brute beasts, in those things they corrupt themselves."*

Apostates corrupt the public standards of society and the personal standards of individuals. These men may have doctorate degrees from highly respected universities, but they are ignorant of the spiritual things of God. They are crafty men having a lot of charisma, but the Scriptures call them brute beasts. Underneath all the wit, personality, and charm, they are ravaging wolves who will stop at nothing to fulfill their wicked desires. Our verse reminds us that they are corrupt themselves.

There are a lot of these brute beasts today in our society. They will spring up a one-name church sign with no doctrinal affiliation attached. They may say they are Baptist in doctrine, but will leave it off the sign, hoping they can reach everyone in the community. They use different versions of the Bible and correct the King James Bible by saying it is outdated. They claim that any preacher who preaches boldly against sin is full of wrath and arrogance. They present a watered-down gospel that requires no repentance, only head knowledge. They never mention being under conviction for salvation or a changed life after conversion. It is "come as you are and leave as you were" at these churches.

I challenge you to look closer at these men whom the Bible calls brute beasts. Examine their teaching, their lives, and their agenda. If a man claims that we have no final authority of the Scriptures and we can use many different versions, please note that he is a wolf in sheep's clothing. When he conceals his doctrine from society to grow a crowd, it reveals his agenda. He is not about ministry, but he is about money. He is not about people, but he is about popularity and prosperity. We cannot allow the brute beasts of our day to rob us of the truth. Stay with what has been tested, tried, and proven!

"Mark These Men"

Jude 11 - "Woe unto them! for they have gone in the way of Cain, and ran greedily after the error of Balaam for reward, and perished in the gainsaying of Core."

The three men in this verse depict apostates. In doctrine, Cain rejected the blood atonement; in desires, Balaam sold out for money; and in disrespect, Core disrespected Moses. You will still find this true about the apostates of our day. They are in error in their teaching and handling of finances, and there is no regard for preachers who preach with authority.

Someone asked me about a group of so-called preachers who loved to mock other men of God. They regularly made it their practice to mock other men's preaching and ministries. I told the individual that if those men were truly saved and did not repent, they would suffer the consequences of their actions. You cannot mock men of God and get by with it. If they continued to mock preachers and suffered no ill effects, then mark it down, they are not saved. These men all claimed to be preachers when, in reality, they were nothing more than apostates. They have never known the truth of God's Word. They do not have the Spirit of God, so they have no fear of God.

We must mark these kinds of men. We cannot afford to be fooled by them or their agenda. Apostates will always be in this world until Christ returns. Real men of God are known for the truth that they preach. They are known for having a spirit of humility and genuine love for God and His people. They are concerned about your soul and not your pocketbook. Thank God for the old-time preachers of the past and the present, who have preached it right and kept it tight down through the years. These are holy men of God who are well-respected and walk with God. They are men who have made their mark on us for the cause of Christ and taught us to mark the apostates of our day.

"Some People Have No Shame"

Jude 12 - *"These are spots in your feasts of charity, when they feast with you, feeding themselves without fear: clouds they are without water, carried about of winds; trees whose fruit withereth, without fruit, twice dead, plucked up by the roots;"*

We have all heard the phrase, "Some people have no shame." This statement is true about apostates. They do not care who they deceive, or who gets hurt, or whose soul they damn to Hell. They will pretend to be a believer and a friend to other believers. Jude says that these people are spots in our feasts of charity. In other words, they may appear to be a child of God, but they are not.

Apostates do not add to the church, but they deceive and destroy. They will feed themselves without fear and have no shame in helping themselves. These people are takers in the work of God and know nothing about the truth. They teach and encourage people to be self-centered. Christianity teaches believers to focus on Christ, then on other believers and a lost world. It is sad how much emphasis the world places on self-image and self-promotion today. I am not saying that everyone who is guilty of self-promotion is an apostate, but apostasy has affected our society and even the atmosphere in our churches.

Apostates are full of empty promises. They cannot benefit or give anything to other believers in any way. They are clouds without water, trees without fruit, twice dead and plucked up by the roots! These people take and have nothing to give in return. We are not to be swayed by their personalities or their popularity. In the end, they will always leave another believer hurting and lacking. Remember, these people have no shame!

"The Great Tsunami"

Jude 13 - *"Raging waves of the sea, foaming out their own shame; wandering stars, to whom is reserved the blackness of darkness for ever."*

Tsunamis are giant waves caused by earthquakes or volcanic eruptions under the sea. In the ocean's depths, tsunami waves do not dramatically increase in height, but as the waves travel inland, they build up to higher and higher heights as the depth of the ocean decreases. Tsunamis are raging waves of the sea that cause massive destruction and death.

Jude declares apostates as the raging waves of the sea. Like tsunamis, they bring massive destruction and spiritual death to those who follow them. Apostates have no shame in the lengths that they will go to propagate their false teaching and doctrine. Jude says they are wandering stars and that God will surely punish them for their false propaganda. We must beware of the apostates of our day. We must hold to the truth, preach the truth, and practice the truth so that others might hear the truth.

Apostates are violent in the sense that they come after your soul. They want to indoctrinate you with false teaching and lead you to death and destruction. They are vile because they do not care about the truth and are not ashamed to pervert it. They despise those who believe in holiness and righteousness.

We see this great tsunami not only in our churches but also in our country today. We all love America, but we do not love what America has become. We are seeing the results of removing God from our schools and court system. We now have a godless society experiencing a great tsunami of apostasy. People no longer care about hearing what is true but what is convenient.

These raging waves will continue to destroy the minds and hearts of the next generation. We must stand against apostates by holding up the banner of truth and proclaiming it louder than ever. If apostates have no shame in their false doctrine, how much more should we, as Christians, have no shame in standing for what we know is right? The truth will still set men free.

"A Bright Word in a Dark Hour"

Jude 14 - *"And Enoch also, the seventh from Adam, prophesied of these, saying, Behold, the Lord cometh with ten thousands of his saints,"*

Sometimes we feel that this world is growing darker by the day. It seems more difficult now to find a bright spot in society. If you turn on the news, listen to the radio, or watch the Internet, you will not find much encouragement in our world today. The world has nothing positive to announce.

The reason is simple: they are in darkness and cannot offer peace without knowing the Prince of Peace. Enoch was living in a very dark day. Society was growing further and further away from God. People were living in sin and enjoying their wickedness, just like today.

Discouragement would have been as easy in Enoch's time as it is in our world today. However, Enoch had a bright word in a dark hour. He received a prophecy that would give hope to his generation and the generations to come in the future. Enoch declared it in his day, and Jude echoed the same words in his time.

Not only did they find a bright word in a dark hour, but you and I, dear reader, can also find encouragement from these words today. The message is clear and simple: Jesus is coming soon! He is coming first in the rapture, and then He will come in the revelation. We, the church, will be taken out of this world, and then God will pour His wrath upon it. He will destroy the satanic trinity, restore the nation of Israel, and redeem this earth from the curse. He will then set up His kingdom for one thousand glorious years.

What a day that will be when Jesus rules here on this earth! The world may look dark now, but a brighter day is coming! With each passing day, we are getting closer to His coming. The reality is that it could happen at any moment. Dear reader, we must be prepared, not just in salvation, but in our service. We must encourage others to be ready and watch for the Lord's return. That is the bright word in a dark hour that we must share with others. We must encourage one another to stay the course and stand on the truth of God's Word. Our focus must be on Christ and Him alone in these last days. Let me remind you that when He comes the second time to this earth, He will be coming with His saints!

"Judgment Day!"

Jude 15 - *"to execute judgment upon all, and to convince all that are ungodly among them of all their ungodly deeds which they have ungodly committed, and of all their hard speeches which ungodly sinners have spoken against him."*

Enoch not only prophesied that Jesus would come again, but when He comes, He will execute judgment upon all the ungodly in this world. They relish in their wickedness and like to boast about the ungodly deeds that they have committed. They enjoy their hard speeches against the God who created them. They take His name in vain and make light of the eternal punishment that awaits them. They curse God and spew out wickedness without fear of the eternal consequences that await them. It may look like these wicked people get by with their sinful living, but this verse reminds us that a reckoning day is coming.

God will set the record straight for all those who have stood against Him. We must warn the sinner of the judgment to come and do our part to bring them to Christ. We were all ungodly at one time and without hope.

I'm thankful to be on the right side of God's judgment. That does not mean that we won't face judgment. We know the Scriptures teach us that we will each stand before God and give a personal account of our lives. However, it makes a big difference when you know the judge! There is peace in knowing your sins were judged at Calvary. There is peace in knowing that the judge of this earth is your dearest friend. It is a blessing to be saved, knowing that we will not face the judgment Jude is speaking about in this verse.

The blood of Jesus Christ has cleansed the child of God from all of our past, present, and future sins. Christ's blood has made us righteous in the eyes of God. Because of His blood, we are not under wrath, but thank God we are under grace. Let us remember that the same hand that brought Israel out of Egypt and across the Red Sea is also the same hand that rolled the waters over Pharaoh and his army. The ungodly will surely face God for every deed they have done and every seed they have sown. As we think about God's judgment in the last days, let us rejoice in our salvation and do all we can to rescue the lost.

"The Profile of an Apostate"

Jude 16 - *"These are murmurers, complainers, walking after their own lusts; and their mouth speaketh great swelling words, having men's persons in admiration because of advantage."*

Jude takes the time to give us a profile of the apostates he has been talking about. He begins by saying that they are murmurers. Think about what it means to murmur. The definition of murmuring is a low and distinct continuous sound. It means to complain in soft, mumbling tones or to grumble.

That is what apostates like to do. They like to sneak around, spewing their deceit and poisoning others in a soft tone. They constantly question the truth to cause others to doubt it. You cannot satisfy someone who is a murmurer. They will always find something to grumble about. That is how apostates begin to reach those they set out to deceive. They cannot build anything up, so they have to tear down what others have built.

They complain to those who will listen. They are constantly looking for someone they can find fault with. They will write articles and produce podcasts debating the truth. They despise the truth and those who live by it.

Jude says they walk after their own lusts, meaning they are all about their own selfish desires. They are not interested in anything that benefits anyone other than themselves. Having the gift of gab, they know how to articulate words. We must be careful not to be swayed by someone who has a great personality and is well-spoken. Listen to what people say rather than be fooled by how they say it. Do not allow their charisma to sweep you off your feet. We must be interested in one thing, which is the truth of God's Word.

The truth does not need to be dressed up or appealing to my flesh in any way. The truth is to be given just as it is, to men as they are, and we have a responsibility to receive it. Jude does an excellent job of giving us the profile of apostates in this verse. You and I will do well to remember this verse of Scripture. Think about all the great preachers God has placed in your life who invested in you and were interested in your soul. We should take a moment and thank God that He has kept us from being deceived.

"Words to Remember"

Jude 17 - *"But, beloved, remember ye the words which were spoken before of the apostles of our Lord Jesus Christ;"*

We hear a lot of chatter in this modern-day world. The internet and social media world have created an atmosphere where people like to voice their ideas and opinions. Most do it without ever considering the consequences of what they are saying. We must remember that God is keeping a record of what we say, and one day we will give an account of those words. Another thought to remember is that a spiritual man or woman is not known by how much they say or how well they say it, but James said it is the ability to bridle their words.

Many of the words we hear daily are not worth remembering or repeating. However, our text reminds us that some words are worth remembering but are often neglected or overlooked. It is the Word of God. The Holy Spirit gave the apostles the words to write, and Jude encourages the saints to remember the Book!

The way to remember the Bible is to read the Bible. You would be surprised at the people who attend church regularly but do not read God's Word. No wonder these people live a defeated life. Friend, if we neglect His Word, we forfeit our right to live in victory. All the answers we will ever need for the questions in our lives are in the pages of the Bible. These are words to remember!

As a pastor, I have watched people and observed that members of the church who read their Bibles know how to face the struggles of life. The Lord brings to their remembrance what they need when facing difficult circumstances. That is why we read God's Word over and over again. The more familiar we become with His Word, the more likely we are to remember His instructions. It is interesting what we can remember at times and what we can forget. Never letting a day pass without reading your Bible should be your goal. Teach your children and grandchildren the importance of reading and memorizing the Scriptures. One final admonishment is to be sure you do not elevate man's words over the Word of God. Do not take counsel from those who have forgotten His Word altogether. Remember His Word!

"God's Men Told Us Right"

Jude 18 - *"how that they told you there should be mockers in the last time, who should walk after their own ungodly lusts."*

Jude reminds us that the apostles predicted that mockers would come in the last days. They were right then, and they are still right today. This world enjoys mocking the things of God. They mock Him through their music and movies, spewing vile and profane words. They laugh at sin, relish in their evil deeds, and curse the name of God because they are ungodly.

Thank God for the men who warned us about these ungodly men walking after their own lusts. Men of God who told the truth are what salvaged the hearts and homes of people sitting in churches across this country! They told us about the penalty of sin and the consequences of not taking heed to the preaching of the Word of God.

Today it is hard to find a place where the preacher loves the Lord enough to tell people the truth. Many so-called preachers have become lovers of their own selves. They are better politicians than they are preachers. We have men who work the crowd and entertain the audience with a short sermon of exhortation. We need men of God who will stand with a heavy burden weighing on their souls and preach with a passion burning deep within their hearts.

God help us to listen to the men who have told us right all these years. We must stay the course and keep preaching the old-time way. God still has men who are preaching the Bible and telling it right. Don't get crossed up with a man of God or leave a church service mad because the preacher laid it out straight and simple. If we are guilty, we must humble ourselves and repent of our sins. God will show us mercy, and we will love the man who told us the truth.

Think about those who have despised the men of God who told it right. Their lives never got better when they walked away from the truth. I want to challenge you to reflect on some of the men of God that He used to preach to your soul. Where would you be if it had not been for those preachers caring enough to tell you what was right? God used them in a special way to help you along life's journey.

"Having Not the Spirit"

Jude 19 - *"These be they who separate themselves, sensual, having not the Spirit."*

In this verse, Jude gives us three marks of these mockers who will appear in the last days. He first says that they will separate themselves. That does not mean they will separate from the world or unbelief as Christians do, but they will separate from true and consecrated Christians. He also marks them by saying that they are sensual. That means that they satisfy their senses by having no moral restrictions. They do whatever will please them and justify their ungodly deeds.

In the last mark given, Jude sums up these apostates as a whole when he says they have not the Spirit. If you have ever wondered how some people can walk away from God and live as wickedly as before, Jude gives us the answer. When people mock the things of God and make light of sacred things with no shame or chastisement, then you can be sure they have not the Spirit.

We live in a day when men who claim to be preachers mock the real men of God. Some might even wonder how they can get by with this kind of mocking. A truly saved person will not get by with it but will suffer chastisement for his behavior. However, if a person can continue through life and face no consequences, you can mark it down that they have not the Spirit. They will one day be held accountable for their wicked mockery at the judgment seat.

Dear friend, do not be deceived by those who claim Christianity but despise holiness and consecration. Do not follow this contemporary movement that teaches you can live worldly and still live victoriously. They may know the words but never experience the power because they have not the Spirit. What a blessing to have been around many real Christians who have been great examples of Christian living. Their lives have taught us to walk humbly and reverently before our God. We should never take His Word or His will lightly. Those with the Spirit of God living inside them know that He is the most sensitive Person they will ever meet. He speaks to us when we do wrong, and He encourages us to live a more holy life for the glory of God. The question for each of us is this, "Do you have the Spirit of God living within you?"

"Praying in the Holy Ghost"

Jude 20 - *"But ye, beloved, building up yourselves on your most holy faith, praying in the Holy Ghost,"*

Here, we have a wonderful admonishment for the beloved. Jude is encouraging the brethren to build themselves up. Now, he is not talking about building up our ego or self-image but our most holy faith by praying in the Holy Ghost. There is no substitute for Spirit-filled praying. Just like we need Spirit-filled singing and preaching, we need men and women who will pray in the Holy Ghost.

What does it mean to pray in the Holy Ghost? It means we pray according to God's will. The Spirit of God helps us to pray the proper prayers. Spiritual men and women know how to pray because they live a surrendered life praying for the things that please Him, not them. They have a desire to see God's will done on earth. They do not try to manipulate God into doing something they desire. Too much of our praying can become about us rather than Him.

When we allow the Spirit to guide us in our praying, it strengthens our faith in God. We learn to pray with confidence and assurance. May God give us more saints who will learn to pray in the Holy Ghost. Dear reader, evaluate your prayer life. Look at your prayer list and ask yourself, "Are these the prayers that the Spirit has led me to pray?"

Begin your prayer time early in the morning. Do not wait until midday or evening. Give God the first part of your day in prayer. Keep your prayer life simple and speak to God sincerely. Do not let your prayer life become mechanical. Keep it fresh by pouring your heart out to God. Keep your secret time a secret from others. Do not share much about your prayer life, but let it be holy and personal between you and your Father. Guard your prayer life, and do not allow Satan to use distractions and defeat to keep you out of the prayer closet. The greatest thing anyone can ever do for someone is to pray for them. Holy Ghost praying will send revival to our land once again. Holy Ghost praying will turn the tide of wickedness in our country and awaken the sleepy saints in our churches. We must determine to keep on praying and believing in these last days.

"An Absolute Must"

Jude 21 - *"keep yourselves in the love of God, looking for the mercy of our Lord Jesus Christ unto eternal life."*

Jude admonishes believers to build their lives on the Word of God, pray in the power of God, and remain in the love of God. If a Christian does the first two things, the last one will come naturally. The Word of God and prayer will keep an individual in the love of God. Our passion for God comes when we fellowship with Him in His Word and prayer. Our pulpits are dry, and our pews are silent because people are too busy and distracted. Think about how hard it is to get people to focus on their walk with God and commit to spending more time with Him. It amazes me how people can pack their schedule full of events and responsibilities, but there is seldom time planned for the Person they claim to love the most.

Dear reader, this verse stands as a reminder that our love for God will only be as strong as we plan for it to be. The more time you spend with someone, it makes you love them more. The more you know someone, the more you will love them. Are you keeping yourself in the love of God? Do not allow work, schedules, hobbies, and events to rule your life. Let your love for Christ be the motivating factor in your life. Remove the frustrations of life by focusing on your relationship with God. I have watched people as they backslide and become easily irritated and critical, slowly growing harder toward life and those around them. They lose their joy, tears, and their attitude of gratitude toward the Lord and His people. They talk about the negative things in life and become less patient with those around them.

What has happened to this individual that was once so joyful? What happened is they lost the love for God that they once had. They may still be serving and attending church, but they have backslidden in their heart, and you can see it in their spirit. The tender, gentle

203

saint that once was a blessing to all has now become someone who will give you a piece of their mind if you cross them. This poor soul is in desperate need of revival. They no longer look for the mercy of our Lord to show to others because they no longer love God as they once did. To receive mercy means we must show mercy toward others. How can we be merciful if we do not have God's love burning within us? I encourage you to make it your priority to keep yourself in the love of God.

"You Can Make a Difference"

Jude 22 - *"And of some have compassion, making a difference:"*

Is it possible for someone like me or you to make a difference? After all, we are just one individual in a world population of approximately eight billion souls. The devil wants us to believe that there is no way we can make an impact in this world or in the world to come. Sadly, many believers have bought into his lies and have blended into society without any burden for those around them. They are perfectly content with letting their family members, neighbors, and those they meet go to Hell. They are living the American dream and will one day leave this world having made no impact in eternity. They are simply living life for number one.

The phrase "and of some" is highlighted in our verse today. Thank God some believe they can make a difference through Christ! They will not sit idly by and let the world go to Hell. They are striving to win souls, encourage saints, and war against the evil forces of Hell in these last days. If you want to know what motivates these faithful few, it's a heart of compassion. Their passion for God has given them a vision for others and has stirred their hearts with compassion like Christ had when He saw the multitudes scattered abroad, about to faint, and as sheep having no shepherd. We need to pray for God to give us a heart of compassion for those around us. We need to see people the way Christ saw them, because that is the only way we will ever make a difference in this world.

Joseph made a difference in Egypt, Daniel made a difference in Babylon, Moses made a difference in the wilderness, Joshua made a difference in Canaan, Jonah made a difference in Nineveh, and you and I can make a difference in our world today.

Our verse doesn't say that all have made a difference, but some have. I don't know about you, but I want to be a part of "the some" who have helped to make a difference in this world. Purpose in your heart that you will help make a difference in someone's life today. Give God your best so you can make a difference. Pray for compassion and look for someone to show the mercy of our Savior to. Ask the Lord to give you wisdom on how to handle and help the people He places in your path. Mark your words and prayerfully consider your actions in front of those around you.

"Be Careful in the Rescue"

Jude 23 - *"and others save with fear, pulling them out of the fire; hating even the garment spotted by the flesh."*

In our verse, we see a great rescue. Someone was almost completely gone, and a brave soul rescued them from the fire. In light of this epistle, Jude speaks about rescuing someone from heresy, maybe a brother or sister who has fallen prey to false teaching and is being led astray by damnable doctrine. We can also make the application concerning a lost person being led astray by these apostates. Their ultimate end is going to be the fire of Hell. False doctrine will lead lost souls straight to Hell. Thank God for every soul rescued from false teaching and the flames of eternal fire.

However, we must not overlook the warning we see in this verse. While trying to help reach others, we must remember ourselves. Please note that the Christian soldiers in our text performed their rescues with extreme caution. They realized they were entering the enemy's territory and knew they were composed of the same weak flesh as those who needed to be delivered. They carried out the rescue with the fearful realization that they could fall into the same ditch. We should not take this caution lightly because we have seen this tragedy happen many times. Have you ever seen someone try to help rescue another individual from false teaching, then end up in it themselves? The rescuer was consumed in the fire of false teaching and false doctrine, being overtaken and becoming a casualty in the rescue mission.

It is my belief that if the previous verses are not applied, the brother attempting to rescue another will become a casualty. Friend, we must be strong in the Word of God, the power of prayer, and have a burning love for God before we can help others. Then we must use extreme caution and recognize the seriousness of helping those led astray. If we fail to approach with fear and trembling, then we are subject to fall. There is a final warning in the process of this rescue. Our garments could get spotted in the process. False teaching may not consume the rescuer, but it can get them off course for life if they are not careful. Be sure you are settled in the Scriptures before you try to rescue others.

"How to Keep From Falling"

Jude 24 - *"Now unto him that is able to keep you from falling, and to present you faultless before the presence of his glory with exceeding joy,"*

If we make it to the end of our journey without falling into sin or false doctrine, it will be all because of Him. To be able to stand in His presence faultless with exceeding joy will also be because of Him. We cannot accomplish either of the truths in this verse by ourselves. Thank God that what we cannot do, He is able to do through us. Relying on ourselves, we would not last one day, but thankfully, He is there to help us.

Whenever I read this verse, I see His help. He keeps us from falling off into the ditches of life. I also see His holiness in this verse. How could we ever stand faultless before Him when we have sinned more after we were saved than we could ever remember? The answer is we will stand in His righteousness and not our own. I also see His honor in this verse. The glory we will share will not be our glory but the glory of our Savior. The verse says, "the presence of His glory." Then I see happiness in this verse. We will rejoice with our Lord on that great and glorious day.

What a blessing to know that we are not keeping ourselves. Dear reader, it would be impossible for us to keep ourselves from the snares and pitfalls of this life. We are no match for Satan, no match for this world, and no match for our wicked flesh, but we do know someone who can defeat them all. Jesus has already conquered these enemies and proven that He has given us victory.

I want to encourage you, child of God, to be faithful to the very end. The victory is ours, and we have the assurance that He will keep us and fulfill His will in our lives. I'm glad the Scriptures teach that we are more than conquerors through Christ Jesus. We will one day stand in His presence and will no longer have to battle this flesh. We will no longer have to deal with Satan or live in a sin-cursed world. Eternity is going to be all about King Jesus! What a day that will be when we stand in His presence and in His likeness! There will be joy in the hearts and on the faces of God's children as our faith ends in sight. The battle will be over, the victory will be ours, and we will enjoy the presence of our Savior for all eternity. Keep looking up, my dear friend, and stay faithful in the fight. Whenever you feel weak, remember He will keep you from falling, and there is a brighter day ahead. It will not be long until we see Him!

"Our Wise God"

Jude 25 - *"to the only wise God our Saviour, be glory and majesty, dominion and power, both now and ever. Amen."*

Our verse is the only place in this epistle where Jude calls our Lord "Savior." Peter used this title five times, but Jude began by reminding us of the common salvation. He now brings it down to the climax for every soul that reads this epistle: Can you call Him your Savior? It is not enough to say that Jesus Christ is "a savior" or "the savior," but we must say, along with Jude in this verse, that He is "our Savior."

He is also the "only wise God." Jude has just dealt with false teachers and their false teaching. He now points us back to the source of all true wisdom. Our God can supply the wisdom we need to live our lives for His glory. He closes this epistle by using some words that honor our wise God.

He uses the word "only," which separates Him from all others. That means He stands alone in His wisdom, and no one can compare to Him. He uses the word "glory," which is the total of all that God is and does. The glory of man is vain and swiftly fades as the grass of this earth. The glory of God endures and lasts for all eternity.

He uses the word "majesty," which means great or magnificent. To praise our God is to praise the most magnificent Person in the universe. He is the God of all gods, the King of all kings, and the Lord of all lords. He is majestic in His person, His character, and His acts.

Jude also uses the word "dominion," which denotes God's sovereignty and rule over everything. The Greek word means "strength or might," but it carries the idea of complete control over all things. He also uses the word "power," which means "authority," which gives Him the right to use the power. All authority belongs to

Jesus Christ (Matt. 28:18), even over the powers of darkness (Eph. 1:19–23). As we yield to Him, we are given the strength and power to accomplish His will for our lives.

This verse is a tremendous doxology given by Jude. Knowing the purpose that this dear servant had in mind when he wrote this letter gives it an even greater significance. He is reminding his readers of the greatness of Jesus Christ. He is reminding us that He is wonderful, majestic, all-powerful, and that He will be the One who is keeping us in the end! If everyone who reads this epistle would realize that, then they would never be led astray by false teachers.

NOTES:

NOTES:

NOTES:

NOTES:

NOTES:

〉